Giving Back

In the series *Asian American History and Culture*,
edited by Cathy Schlund-Vials, Shelley Sang-Hee Lee,
and Rick Bonus. Founding editor, Sucheng Chan;
editors emeriti, David Palumbo-Liu, Michael Omi,
K. Scott Wong, and Linda Trinh Võ.

ALSO IN THIS SERIES:

Manan Desai, *The United States of India: Anticolonial Literature and Transnational Refraction*
Cathy J. Schlund-Vials, Guy Beauregard, and Hsiu-chuan Lee, eds., *The Subject(s) of Human Rights: Crises, Violations, and Asian/American Critique*
Malini Johar Schueller, *Campaigns of Knowledge: U.S. Pedagogies of Colonialism and Occupation in the Philippines and Japan*
Crystal Mun-hye Baik, *Reencounters: On the Korean War and Diasporic Memory Critique*
Michael Omi, Dana Y. Nakano, and Jeffrey T. Yamashita, eds., *Japanese American Millennials: Rethinking Generation, Community, and Diversity*
Masumi Izumi, *The Rise and Fall of America's Concentration Camp Law: Civil Liberties Debates from the Internment to McCarthyism and the Radical 1960s*
Shirley Jennifer Lim, *Anna May Wong: Performing the Modern*
Edward Tang, *From Confinement to Containment: Japanese/American Arts during the Early Cold War*
Patricia P. Chu, *Where I Have Never Been: Migration, Melancholia, and Memory in Asian American Narratives of Return*
Cynthia Wu, *Sticky Rice: A Politics of Intraracial Desire*
Marguerite Nguyen, *America's Vietnam: The* Longue Durée *of U.S. Literature and Empire*
Vanita Reddy, *Fashioning Diaspora: Beauty, Femininity, and South Asian American Culture*
Audrey Wu Clark, *The Asian American Avant-Garde: Universalist Aspirations in Modernist Literature and Art*
Eric Tang, *Unsettled: Cambodian Refugees in the New York City Hyperghetto*
Jeffrey Santa Ana, *Racial Feelings: Asian America in a Capitalist Culture of Emotion*

A list of additional titles in this series appears at the back of this book.

L. Joyce Zapanta Mariano

GIVING BACK

Filipino America and the Politics of Diaspora Giving

TEMPLE UNIVERSITY PRESS
Philadelphia • Rome • Tokyo

TEMPLE UNIVERSITY PRESS
Philadelphia, Pennsylvania 19122
tupress.temple.edu

Published 2021

Library of Congress Cataloging-in-Publication Data

Names: Mariano, L. Joyce Zapanta, 1973– author.
Title: Giving back : Filipino America and the politics of diaspora giving / L. Joyce Zapanta Mariano.
Other titles: Asian American history and culture.
Description: Philadelphia : Temple University Press, 2021. | Series: Asian American history and culture | Includes index. | Summary: "Examines Filipino diaspora through the complex of meanings associated with "giving back" and explores the process of diaspora formation. Argues that giving-related institutions and discourse-such as aid, development, altruism, and benevolence-are integral to understanding diaspora formation today"—Provided by publisher.
Identifiers: LCCN 2020013294 (print) | LCCN 2020013295 (ebook) | ISBN 9781439918395 (cloth) | ISBN 9781439918401 (paperback) | ISBN 9781439918418 (pdf)
Subjects: LCSH: Filipino Americans—Charitable contributions. | Emigrant remittances—Philippines. | Filipinos—United States—Social conditions. | Charities—Philippines. | Filipino diaspora.
Classification: LCC E184.F4 M363 2021 (print) | LCC E184.F4 (ebook) | DDC 305.899/21073—dc23
LC record available at https://lccn.loc.gov/2020013294
LC ebook record available at https://lccn.loc.gov/2020013295

♾ The paper used in this publication meets the requirements of the American National Standard for Information Sciences—Permanence of Paper for Printed Library Materials, ANSI Z39.48-1992

Printed in the United States of America

9 8 7 6 5 4 3 2 1

To my father, Manuel J. Mariano

Contents

Acknowledgments

It would be too much to hope that this book could match the generosity of the people who have given me so much of their time. I never took it for granted that I would finish college, much less graduate school and this book, and I am deeply humbled by those who encouraged me to persevere through their example, kindness, and support. I cannot help but reflect on those times that I felt in over my head or dragged down by self-doubt, yet there was always someone who helped me remember why I cared about this project and emboldened me to finish. I use those moments to guide my acknowledgments, which are nevertheless woefully incomplete.

I have been in interdisciplinary institutional spaces my entire career, and the critiques facilitated by interdisciplinary self-reflexivity continue to challenge my research, teaching, and understanding of the academy. Roderick Ferguson and Jennifer Pierce helped me see that an interdisciplinary cultural studies program would best serve the questions that propelled me toward graduate school. I am grateful to have learned from and with fellow graduate students in the American Studies Department and my cross-disciplinary cohort in the MacArthur Program at the University of Minnesota: Sonjia, Marie, Josh, Sharon, Hoku, Fernando, Amy, Kate, and many others. This book began with my dissertation, which I wrote sitting across from Sonjia Hyon. Marie Sulit encouraged me toward my first conference presentations. Even though it has been many years, I am still surprised that Josephine Lee, Jigna Desai, Erika Lee, Doug Hartmann, Teresa Swartz, and the great David Noble agreed to work with me despite my quirks and inadequacies. Jo Lee never ceases to make me tear up, in the good way, when I see her at conferences.

If not for the intellectual community and models of professional integrity I found when I was a lecturer at DePaul University and the University of Illinois, Chicago, I would not have had it in me to finish. I am grateful for friendships with and the examples set by Billy Johnson Gonzalez, Laura Kina, Camilla Fojas, Lourdes Torres, Amina Chaudhri, Ann Russo, Francesca Royster, Lori Pierce, Anna Guevarra, and Karen Su. My Chicago work sessions with Sarah Koning and Megan Wheelehan were also a lifeline.

I think about what I call "my magical postdoc year" in the Department of Asian American Studies at the University of Illinois, Urbana-Champaign, with frequency, fondness, and gratitude. Sandra Ruiz, Christina Chin, Ahalya Satkunaratnam, Lisa Cacho, Fiona Ngô, and Mireya Loza helped me find joy, as well as my arguments. I wrote this book with Isabela Quintana both virtually and physically by my side. I cannot thank Mimi Thi Nguyen and Martin Manalansan enough for helping me carry it through to the end. Their integrity, thoughtful mentorship, and generous friendship serve as models for the kind of academic I strive to be.

Often with my feet to the fire, I presented each chapter and almost every section at the American Studies Association and Association for Asian American Studies conferences. I marvel at how relationships that began amid fabric wall partitions in undifferentiated hotel conference rooms have transformed from fleeting interactions to cherished sources of mentorship and intellectual exchange. I am thankful to be a part of unpretentious and politically committed communities. Multiple panels with Gina Velasco and Harrod Suarez inspired me. The feedback, questions, and insight from Augusto Espiritu, Sarita See, Rick Bonus, Lucy Burns, Josen Diaz, Robyn Rodriguez, Theo Gonzalves, Nerissa Balce, and Allan Isaac have also been particularly invaluable to me.

I thank the faculty in American Studies Department at the University of Hawai'i, Mānoa (UH), for their support: Bill Chapman, Betsy Colwill, Jonna Eagle, Vernadette Gonzalez, Noelle Kahanu, Karen Kosasa, Brandy Nālani McDougal, Dennis Ogawa, Robert Perkinson, Kath Sands, David Stannard, Joe Stanton, Jeff Tripp, and Mari Yoshihara. There are many others at UH who have worked with me in writing groups, extended their collegiality, and provided me with spaces to share my work: Brian Chung, Hokulani Aikau, Lisa Uperesa, Pia Arboleda, Vina Lanzona, Cindy Franklin, Colin Moore, Myungji Yang, Lee Ann Wang, and Jennifer Darrah. I remain grateful to Vernadette for reaching out to me while I was in the job market and for continuing to help me navigate through the choppy waters of academia. Mari always makes time for me when I pop in with random questions, often without context or preamble, about publishing, ideas for future research, and music, and I have greatly benefited from her reading of last-minute proposals and drafts. My working partnership with Brian has been fundamental to my sanity and has made me a better colleague and friend.

I thank Robyn Rodriguez for helping me work through the goals of each chapter at a crucial time in the process. I am indebted to Anita Mannur for her patience and keen editor's eye in working with me on the article that became Chapter 1 of this book. Lauren Yamaguchi was my research assistant for a couple of months and a most welcome diversion from what would have been a lonely summer in my office. Before I even knew what this book was really about, I began conversations with Temple University Press. I am thrilled to have had the chance to work with my series editor, Rick Bonus, and am grateful for his feedback, encouragement, and cheer. The brutal final push to completing the book was made bearable by the people who worked to understand my hurdles and never failed to ask how they could help. I am grateful to Lucy Burns, Isabela Quintana, Brian Chung, and Martin Manalansan for always checking in on how the writing was going.

The thinking, exploration, and research for this book led me to many places in the continental United States, Hawaii, and the Philippines. In Washington, D.C., Los Angeles, San Francisco, San Jose, New York City, Atlanta, Honolulu, Minneapolis, Chicago, Manila,

Quezon City, Makati, Olongapo, Angono, and Marinduque, I benefited from acts of kindness, sometimes from complete strangers. So many people took time to speak to me about their relationship to the Philippines and their endeavors. I am grateful in particular to Jeremaiah Opiniano, at the inception of the project, and Ninotchka Rosca, in the final stages of research, for helping me understand their lifework and commitments. Family in California and the Philippines housed me, fed me, and drove me around; my thanks go to Auntie Susan, Uncle Arthur, Auntie Pat, Ate Tina, Ate Jing, Auntie Vi, Auntie Nilda, and Miranda. I also thank my parents, Manny and Lily Mariano. The seed of this project began with my father. Every part of this book is imprinted with his memory, influence, and boundless love.

Last, Kate Kane has lived with this project as long as I have. There is nothing I have accomplished in the past twenty years that is not marked by her support, intelligence, patience, and love. She and Emilia are simply the best.

Giving Back

Introduction

"Charity Begins at Home"

Filipino Americans give back, not only to families in the Philippines but also to communities, projects, and organizations. Filipino Americans may give back to provide relief to poor or vulnerable Filipinos or to address the forces that maintain poverty, vulnerability, or exploitative relationships in the Philippines. These various acts of giving provide a source of cohesion and purpose for Filipino America. Jocelyn Alvarez, for example, a community organizer and president of her Filipino American regional association, describes her relationship to charitable giving:

> Philippine culture is very important. We should all value charity because if you are charitable, it comes back to you many times. It's payback. Charity should always be a part because no matter what, that feeling of sharing is something that makes you complete. It gives you meaning. We as a people have a beautiful way of sharing and community that is sometimes lacking in America.[1]

Giving back, a prominent feature of Filipino American identity and communities, is central to the moral economies of Filipino migration, immigration, and diasporic return.

Efforts to participate in the social development of the Philippines or to improve the lives of Filipinos in the Philippines have become more visible over the past several decades. This is a result of both the increasing flow of economic globalization and the post-1965 migration of Filipino professionals to the United States. These immigrants' personal and financial situations have allowed them to organize and participate in philanthropic, charitable, and social-development projects.[2] The rise in the promotion of philanthropy and its frequency within Filipino America coincides with a global shift in governance that pushes the burdens of social welfare away from state governments and onto private organizations and individuals.[3] This privatization of public welfare ensures the precarity of poor people, whose welfare is left to the whims of donors and the cycles of large foundations, but it also broadens the realm of social responsibility for those with ties to a particular place.[4] Filipino Americans accept at least a degree of this responsibility in the Philippines, as evidenced by the prominence of giving back in Filipino American association newsletters, Filipino American newspapers, and community achievement awards.

While Filipino Americans pursue opportunities to support projects in the Philippines and cultivate a culture of giving back, broader claims about economic development on national and international levels can make instrumental use of these personal and community efforts. State bodies within the Philippine government; regional financial organizations such as the Asian Development Bank; and multilateral institutions, including the World Bank, engage in dialogue, promote policies, and create legislation "targeting diasporas as development actors."[5] In other words, the desire and action on the part of migrants and immigrants to help improve the futures of their respective countries of origin are seen as significant enough to warrant coordinated efforts to guide potential results toward the interests of national economies and the first world's coordination of the global economy. By targeting migrants and immigrants as development actors, these state and financial bodies recode "giving back" to the Philippines in terms of national development, as an international political and economic phenomenon. Giving practices are central to contemporary expressions of Filipino American diasporic belonging and subjectivity, and it is through giving back that Filipino Americans are recruited as development actors and participants in the development regimes of the Philippines. Once they are recruited, the realm of giving back takes on new resonance in contemporary Filipino America.

Filipino Americans have created hundreds of charity, social-development, philanthropic, humanitarian, and social-movement organizations that support ongoing projects in the Philippines. Additionally, Filipino American student and social groups, alumni charters, professional organizations, hometown and regional associations, and fraternal clubs—the variety of social groupings that are commonplace among Asian, Caribbean, and other racialized migrant and immigrant populations—initiate small-scale projects in the Philippines through the donations and organizing efforts of their members. While this is not necessarily their primary or founding mission, they give back to the Philippines as a Filipino American group. For example, the St. Luke's Alumni Nursing Foundation USA raises money to support an endowed scholarship for its members' alma mater in Quezon City. The Filipino American Association of Central New Jersey holds charity balls and golf tournaments to support the Alouette Foundation of the Philippines, which serves underprivileged children in Pasay City. The New Orleans Filipino American Lions Club collects surplus textbooks from the New Orleans school district to donate to elementary schools in Batangas and La Union. Filipinos from Rizal and San Pablo City in Laguna now living in the United States and Canada formed Seven Lakes International to work with the San Pablo City mayor and community organizations to fund local development initiatives, including the construction of facilities to produce oil and fiber from coconuts. Thousands of medical missions to the Philippines have been organized, many led by doctors who trained in the Philippines, immigrated to the United States, and now return to the Philippines to provide surgical, medical, and dental services with groups such as the Philippine American Medical Mission Foundation of Michigan, Aloha Medical Mission, and Philippine Medical Society of Northern California. The vast majority of the Filipino American groups I have come across call out to members and the broader public to provide assistance whenever natural disasters erupt in the Philippines.

Filipino Americans, not unlike other diasporic populations who initiate projects and programs in countries of origin, are called on by homeland governments, national cultures, international nongovernmental organizations (NGOs), and religious institutions to give back. The desire and drive to give back to the Philippines can feel universal in certain segments of Filipino America, so much so that giving-related practices and concerns—and the bonds maintained through giving—infuse what it means to be Filipino in America. The risk, however, is in perceiving the act of giving back as its own end—as proof in and of itself that Filipino Americans remain "Filipino" in their hearts because they choose to give. Erased are the consequences of the ways that giving is imagined and responsibility is placed and the existence of gross inequalities and their global reproduction. Pushing against an understanding of giving back's self-evident goodness and the blind spots that accompany its ubiquity, this book explores the cultural, social, economic, and political conditions of giving back.

I use "diaspora giving" to name the centrality of giving back in Filipino diaspora formation and the questions and analysis that emerge from this focus. The bonds and obligations that give meaning to the Filipino American diaspora do not exist outside culture or history; instead, they are implicated in a complex web of power relationships and conflicting identities. Metaphors, customs, laws, and subjectivities related to giving practices and institutions bind Filipino Americans as a diaspora—and also in relationship to homeland, to Filipinos in the Philippines, to Filipinos in other diasporic nodes, and to each other.

The centrality of giving relationships to social forms and values is explored at length in Marcel Mauss's foundational essay *The Gift: The Form and Reason for Exchange in Archaic Societies.*[6] Mauss's work is vital within the fields of sociology and anthropology; it elaborates how the exchange of gifts involves "the totality of society and its institutions," which are "phenomena [that] are at the same time juridical, economic, religious, and even aesthetic and morphological."[7] Mauss begins his essay with a study of "archaic" societies but concludes with an extension of his "general theory of obligation"—to reciprocate, to give, and to receive—in his own interwar time. Mauss identifies a paradox related to giving in which the giver must *choose* the obligation or duty to give, which he describes as "the atmosphere of the gift, where obligation and liberty intermingle."[8] Elaborating on the undertheorization of solidarity in Maussian scholarship, bioethicist and sociologist Simone Bateman explains, "Indeed, whereas giving (as opposed to selling) is usually perceived as a voluntary, disinterested, and spontaneous form of exchange, it is fundamentally an obligation because giving expresses the ties that bind us to others."[9] In the words of Mary Douglas, who writes in the foreword to the 1990 translation of *The Gift*, "A gift that does nothing to enhance solidarity is a contradiction."[10] A gift seen to be pure and free is a contradiction because it attempts to extract the gift from the chains of obligation, putting "the act of giving outside any mutual ties."[11]

Filipino studies scholars address the contradictions of the gift and the obligations of Filipino migrants most predominantly through remittance giving—money from Filipinos living and working outside the Philippines sent to family members in the Philippines to make consumer purchases, build homes, create small businesses, and pay for educational or health expenses. These scholars illustrate the contradictions of remittances in relationship to a Philippine national culture that celebrates Filipinos' willingness to work abroad so they can send back a portion of their earnings to float the national economy.[12] Many scholars, notably including sociologists Robyn Magalit Rodriguez, Anna Romina Guevarra, and Rhacel Salazar Parreñas, have written about remittances and the dependence on overseas migrant labor in sustaining the Philippine national economy.[13] As these authors show, the Philippines produces the structures that facilitate the migration of Filipinos to work outside the country and to give back through remittances from abroad. These obligations work together in transnational Filipino subjectivities, whether or not one actually secures an opportunity to work abroad, and in the celebration of Filipino labor migrants by the Philippine government for their mobility and their remittance giving, a biopolitics that undergirds global capitalism and the Philippines' role in the global order.[14] Any work on giving back to the Philippines by Filipino Americans must account for the obligations of migrant laborers to give back through remittances.[15] Because charitable, philanthropic, and social-development giving is usually perceived as voluntary, particularly in comparison to the history and culture of remittance giving, there is, perhaps, an even greater risk of understanding giving to recipients outside one's family, or nonremittance giving, as disconnected from both the logics of global capitalism and the Philippine remittance economy.[16]

Filipino Americans work to address the social, economic, and environmental challenges facing the Philippines, and this book takes an interdisciplinary approach to reveal how power operates through the personal, institutional, and economic character of those desires and efforts. *Giving Back: Filipino America and the Politics of Diaspora Giving* examines narratives, representations, and practices of giving back not only in but also about Filipino America diaspora, occurring within and against nationalisms that shape the terms of diasporic belonging for Filipino immigrants and migrants. It understands Filipino American diaspora to be produced in part through U.S. and Philippine state policies and histories regarding migration, citizenship, labor, and racial formation and in relation to other diasporic nodes and trajectories. It analyzes project descriptions, mission statements, organization reports, newsletters, participant observations, and personal and group interviews related to giving back for the frameworks of social transformation that they offer—narratives of multiple and simultaneous homes, identities, and obligations, their meanings and materiality. As visions of society's betterment or advancement, project descriptions and mission statements delineate an organization's choices regarding the best way to help or serve the Philippines or fellow Filipinos; examining frameworks of social transformation and mobility illuminates the logics informing those politics. I do not read frameworks of social transformation and mobility as proof of a migrant's or expatriate's continued love of the homeland but rather as signals of how distance, migration, memory, place, and time translate and inform one's ideas about responsibility and obligation. Alongside materials from Filipino Americans and Filipino American organizations that pursue projects in the Philippines, I analyze writing on diasporic return in policy and personal narratives that prominently feature giving back to comment on the cultural, social, economic, and political dimensions and implications of their representations of giving, migration, and return. Conceived in this way, they narrativize the subject, object, and processes of both diaspora and giving.

"Charity Begins at Home"

The Philippines has made strong ideological and institutional investments in the reproduction of transnational subjectivities, partly through a Filipino population that is willing to work abroad to send back remittances. The ways in which Filipino Americans situate their giving offers a lens through which to analyze diaspora formation under global capitalism. Giving back also creates opportunities for Filipino Americans to shape the terms of diasporic belonging. To build toward these analytical concerns, I turn to the repeated use of the expression "charity begins at home" to describe and elaborate on the centrality of giving back to the moral economies of the Filipino American diaspora.

"Charity begins at home," biblical in origins, is a common expression in general musings about ethical traditions and altruism. It can serve as demand or admonishment, as a stern reminder that we were all once the beneficiaries of someone else's care, and requires a performance of charitability to demonstrate respect of lasting bonds. In another way, acts described as "assistance" or "help" may also operate as a form of claims making by the giver, an insistence that one retains her place in a family or community or nation despite the passage of time, distance, or lack of communication if she abides by a culture of giving.

The expression's incorporation of "home" lends itself well to Filipino American musings about the Philippine "homeland" and the obligations of Filipino Americans to give to those "back home." From my interviews with Filipino American founders, presidents, and leaders of U.S.-based organizations (both informal and registered) that support projects in the Philippines, two particular respondents stand out for their use of "charity begins at home." Instead of justification for *why* they, Filipino American immigrants, choose to focus their activist and philanthropic work in the Philippines (as the place where charity begins), these respondents use the expression to introduce the significance of giving back in the Filipino American diaspora and, importantly, to frame their own interventions in dominant or exclusionary giving practices in diaspora.

Lydia Tanguilig, a Minnesota-based Filipino immigrant, organizes a group of mostly professional Filipino Americans like herself to connect with Philippine-based community organizations. Tanguilig and other members make trips to the Philippines to learn how partner community organizations frame the problems they face, which are often related to livelihood, safety, and access to everyday necessities. Filipino American members report back to the group on what they learned about community organizations' projects and needs in the Philippines, and the group makes decisions about how to support these community organizations in the Philippines. In addition to the knowledge gained from these trips, the Filipino American group holds learning sessions about U.S.-Philippine relations and history and Philippine political economy to make informed and purposeful decisions for the group's time and resources.

Over a shared meal at a restaurant in the Twin Cities, Tanguilig discussed the Philippine-related mission and goals of her group with me. She critiqued Filipino American giving in general terms, situating the goals of her group as an alternative: "Unfortunately, Filipinos here always say charity begins at home, and that means supporting families. . . . We don't want to deliver charity in the Philippines. We want to work with the people."[17] Tanguilig identifies the obligation of many Filipino migrants and immigrants who live and work abroad to support family members in the Philippines. As the literature on Filipino migration and labor documents, this obligation infuses contemporary Filipino society and culture, whether one lives in the Philippines or outside its borders. Tanguilig bemoans this obligation to family as a social norm within transnational Filipino culture because it narrows the extent and practice of giving back.

The social norm to support one's family or contribute to a family household is not usually deemed "unfortunate," even if migrants and immigrants may resent or be overwhelmed by the pressure to remit.[18] However, this resentment is not the locus of Tanguilig's critique. In her estimation, the dominance of remittance giving comes at the expense of other potential bonds in migration, such as the grassroots, community-level efforts in which her group participates. While Tanguilig did not clarify her critique of charity in the interview, many arguments against charity are consistent with her framing of her group as an alternative to remittances as the dominant form of giving back. Common ethical arguments against charity as an institution include how charity works to alleviate symptoms but not root causes of social problems and how charity depends on the donors' understanding of social needs and disregards those of the potential recipients. Tanguilig's brief presentation of giving back, with its focus on working with Philippine communities in person instead of dictating what they need from afar, seems to speak to both arguments. Tanguilig uses "charity begins at home" to illustrate the existence and critique of a giving norm within the Filipino American diaspora. Thus, Tanguilig frames her group as offering an alternative giving practice, and in so doing, she shines a light on what is commonplace and expected to expose what she sees as a roadblock to diasporic participation in a broader vision of social transformation for the Philippines.

Geraldine Bigay, a Filipino immigrant living in the Atlanta area, also acknowledges a normative element in "charity begins at home," offering a critique of dominant "Filipinoness" in giving practices and transnational communities. "In an organization, it's a tendency for individuals to want to overextend," says Bigay. "But charity begins at home. For us that is Bicol [a region in the Philippines]."[19] Bigay connects "charity begins at home" to her alienation from Filipino America and to the rationale for starting her own organization to give back to the Philippines on her own terms. Home, in Bigay's understanding, refers not to the Philippines but to Bicol, the respondent's home region in the central Philippines. Bigay explains that she once belonged to a broad Filipino American association in the Atlanta area but left the group after experiencing the exclusions of ethnic, linguistic, racial, and class norms of belonging within Filipino America: "The other Filipinos pushed us [Bicolanos] out of the Filipino group because we didn't speak Tagalog and a bunch of us married Thai men. We want to create projects for Bicol anyway."[20]

Bigay references an assumption that Filipino migrants and immigrants in the United States, particularly those who are middle class, can speak or at least understand Tagalog, the historical language of the capital region and the basis of the Filipino language.[21] These assumptions can be understood in terms of Filipino migrant history in the United States—early twentieth-century migrants largely came from Ilokano- and Visayan-speaking regions, whereas many of the immigrants who are professionals and their families who came to the United States through the 1965 immigration legislation migrated from Tagalog regions. For these and related reasons, Tagalog has since become associated with upward mobility and educational attainment, which contributes to Bigay's alienation from the broad Filipino American association in Atlanta and from normative Filipinoness in the United States.[22] Faced with racism and regional/linguistic hierarchies within her Filipino American community, Bigay cofounded an organization that supports medical and dental missions, creates and funds scholarships for priests, and establishes libraries, all in her home province of Bicol.

These two examples demonstrate that Filipino Americans understand giving back as part of larger traditions—they both use the expression "charity begins at home." Lydia Tanguilig and Geraldine Bigay draw on personal and community resources to support community organizations in the Philippines and confront issues of access and inequality in the Philippines. Issues related to remittance economies, social responsibility, and cultural nationalism surface in these exchanges about their respective organizational missions and founding moments. But the reverse is also true: issues and histories related to global capitalism, the migration of both labor migrants and Filipino American immigrants, and the difficulties of migration and of homeland return can be examined through the close study of Filipino Americans giving back to the Philippines.

The following section brings together multiple histories to narrate U.S.-Philippine relations and the capitalist bases of largesse in relationship to the postwar multilateral and bilateral programs of official development implemented by the first world and imposed on the third. Giving back from Filipino America bears the trace of all these histories, which undergird the subjectivities produced through giving-related institutions and discourse. The history of Filipino American migration and immigration begins with the colonization of the Philippines by the United States. Because of the "underdevelopment [in the Philippines] that has resulted as a consequence of neocolonialism and the active role the neocolonial state would eventually play in both promoting and facilitating out-migration," contemporary migration and diasporic return must also be understood as the legacy of U.S. colonialism.[23] In the political debate regarding the fate of the Philippines following the colonial exchange and the signing of the Treaty of Paris of 1898, in which Spain ceded to the United States its dominion over the Philippines, Puerto Rico, and Guam, as well as control over the process of independence of Cuba, virtues of charity and obligation were, paradoxically, used to justify territorial expansion and the violence of the Philippine-American War for the American public. Giving back from Filipino America to the Philippines does not overcome histories of colonialism and imperialism that produced desires, relationships, and metaphors of giving between the United States and the Philippines, which cathect in the contemporary moment through development and the developmentalist logics that shape Filipino American subjectivities.[24] This book connects giving back to those histories and works to reckon with the imperialist relations in which it is entangled.

"It Is Not True That Charity Begins at Home": Charity, Development, and Philanthropy and the Global Order

In a speech to the Senate in 1900, Senator Albert Beveridge, one of Washington's most ardent advocates of U.S. overseas expansion, inverted the conventional meaning of "charity begins at home": "It is not true that charity begins at home. . . . Selfishness begins there; but charity begins abroad and ends in its full glory in the home."[25] The charitable opportunity prompting this speech was U.S. colonial control over the Philippines, acquired in 1898 following America's victory in the Spanish-American War. During the first stage of the Philippine-American War, which eventually resulted in more than one million Filipino civilian casualties according to some estimates, Beveridge and fellow pro-imperialists attempted to reconcile overseas expansion and military colonial violence across the Pacific with American liberty and democracy, articulating ideals related to the virtuous exceptionalism of the country to a professed benevolence that would characterize its version of empire.[26] The American colonial project in the Philippines, they argued, sought to develop the country and deliver it from centuries of colonial misrule by Spain. To refuse America's own duty to develop Philippine institutions and infrastructure and guide the Filipino people toward modernity would be, in Beveridge's words, "selfishness." As America stood on the international stage, ready to claim its authority as a colonial master set apart from the cruelty of the European model, "charity" was used as a unifying principle for the American nation.

The relationship with the Philippines was established through charitable exchange, offering American-style development and institutions in the Philippines and, in exchange, receiving glory and comfort in the righteousness of its world leadership. Those who study U.S. colonial history in the Philippines or the cultural politics of American empire often remind us of Beveridge's bold pro-imperialist politics, frequently paired with denouncements of President William McKinley's policy of benevolent assimilation, in their scholarly critiques of racialized modernity and colonial social formations. Beveridge's most oft-quoted passage in this literature demonstrates the ease with which he justifies the colonization of the Philippines through empire's access to new markets, gendered claims to property, and entitlements of whiteness and racial subjection, as well as the duties and burdens of civilization:

> The Philippines are ours forever, "territory belonging to the United States," as the Constitution calls them. And just beyond the Philippines are China's illimitable markets. We will not retreat from either. We will not repudiate our duty in the archipelago. We will not abandon our opportunity in the Orient. We will not renounce our part in the mission of our race, trustee, under God, of the civilization of the world. And we will move forward to our work, not howling our regrets like slaves whipped to their burdens, but with gratitude for a task worthy of our strength, and thanksgiving to Almighty God that He has marked us as His chosen people, henceforth to lead in the regeneration of the world.[27]

Beveridge's speech puts into context how the historic use of "charity begins at home" could be used to rally white Americans to see their colonial relationship to the Philippines as an honorable duty, even when and where such a duty must be forcibly imposed in the pursuit of market expansion and profit.

This imposition of charity was inseparable from empire as a racial project. Drawing on the racial discourses readily accessible to the American public at that time, Beveridge extols the virtues of a country willing to use violence to rescue the people of the Philippines, whose inability to consent to their colonial submission was proof of their savagery:

> The rule of liberty that all just government derives its authority from the consent of the governed, applies only to those who are capable of self-government. We govern the Indians without their consent, we govern our territories without their consent, and we govern our children without their consent. How do they know what our government would be without their consent? Would not the people of the Philippines prefer the just, humane, civilizing government of this Republic to the savage, bloody rule of pillage and extortion from which we have rescued them?[28]

These justifications require the Philippines to be read through the absence of modern and democratic institutions to enable a benevolent American mission alongside the violence of colonialism. Written as benevolence, self-interested but also charitable, the contradictions of the giving exchange are clear. To enable the declaration of an American charitable impulse toward the Philippines, Beveridge relied on the work of "civilization" to locate Filipinos and the Philippines as among the world's savage in both human evolution and territory.[29] This colonial discourse incites white Americans to imagine the Philippines in the same way as the New World, as populated by a people incapable of self-governance, of a territory that was valuable for resource extraction and access to new markets. Charity brings abstract citizens together into nations, constructing home or the domestic in relation to foreign spaces populated by the colonial other, even when territorial divisions between domestic and foreign are obscured, such as in the forced governance of Native Americans.

The usefulness of Beveridge and his discursive and rhetorical address in studies of American empire in the current literature can be broadly characterized by three primary emphases. Scholars draw from Beveridge's oratory and editorial oeuvre to build claims regarding the role of Asia and the Pacific in establishing American-style development and modernization, particularly in terms of territorial expansion, but also in facilitating access to international markets for American goods and capital.[30] Scholars use Beveridge to theorize empire through the intersections of racial formation, American colonial encounters, and the politics of immigration.[31] Scholars also emphasize the mutual constitution of American and Filipino subjects and spaces simultaneously racialized, gendered, and sexualized in American empire.[32]

These takeaways from the literature can also be addressed to social processes that endure and inform the relationships produced in giving and that motivate "the gift." Historian Renato Constantino famously writes in his essay "The Miseducation of the Filipino" that "the most eloquent testimony to the success of the education for colonials which we have undergone" is the enduring myth of America's altruism.[33] The faith in America as the "altruistic benefactor" replaces American economic interests in the Philippines, the history of Philippine resistance to American force, and the carnage of the Philippine-American War in the education of Filipinos.[34] Colonial formations transform in reach and scale in their contemporary presence. International relationships shaped in official development programs extend and retool the rhetorical strategies, spatialities, and temporalities of colonial rule. Forces that lead to the underdevelopment of the Philippines and structure the global order are covered over or softened by official development and contribute to the discourses that mobilize diasporic populations toward developmentalist goals.

The idea of official development was born in the post–World War II "project of intervention in the 'third world' that emerged in the context of decolonization and the cold war."[35] The institutions of official development such as the World Bank and the International Monetary Fund (IMF) were shaped through their professed responsibility "for ensuring a more just and equitable world order," subjecting third-world nations and their perceived political, economic, and cultural precariousness to the standards of progress and modernity achieved by the West.[36] Official development named and measured developing countries and proposed solutions to poverty in terms of economic growth, imposing programs of structural adjustment to stimulate export industries and deregulate financial sectors under the guidance of the World Bank and IMF. These institutions regarded macrolevels of poverty as a stage of development or a "state of undevelopment," dehistoricizing poverty as integral to postcolonial capitalist relations, even in its perpetuation.[37]

Observing the failure of official development programs, international and multilateral agencies now herald migrants and immigrants as the new development actors of the twenty-first century. Researchers working for multilateral labor and financial organizations and scholars across the disciplines have taken up issues related to diaspora development, citing the potential of giving back to homelands in the economies that circulate between homelands and diasporas.[38] In working groups, conferences, policy papers, partnerships, and organizational structure of the United Nations, the World Bank, the Organisation for Economic Co-operation and Development, the United States Agency for International Development (USAID), and the Asian Development Bank, political and economic agencies tout diasporas as "a potent force for development for their countries of origin."[39] The World Bank, for example, maintains a unit implemented "to monitor and forecast remittance and migration flows, and to provide timely analysis on topics such as remittances, migration, and diaspora issues."[40]

The Global Development Professionals Network, a partnership between the *Guardian* newspaper and the Bill and Melinda Gates Foundation, contributes to the international representation of diaspora in the global imaginary: "Diaspora-driven development aims to explore how diaspora groups are gaining more traction as development actors."[41] USAID recognizes diaspora communities as "potentially powerful actors in international affairs and foreign assistance," using categories such as "diaspora philanthropy," "diaspora volunteerism," and the curiously named "diaspora tourism and nostalgic trade" in its organizational materials.[42] It includes diasporas among its list of "working partnerships," a prospective community-based opportunity for development: "Diasporas represent a vast and diverse community that have not only powered the development of the United States, but also hold the potential for transforming developing countries around the world. . . . Whether growing businesses in India, responding to a disaster in Haiti, or supporting peacebuilding efforts in Liberia, diasporas have a uniquely important role in addressing diplomatic, development and humanitarian challenges abroad."[43] Here is a slight shift in the multicultural discourse that has historically celebrated the contributions of immigrants to various labor sectors and industries of the United States. Instead of immigrants, it is the diasporans who power the economic growth of the country while simultaneously holding "the potential for transforming developing countries around the world." Diaspora development, in other words, is the incorporation of diasporic-giving subjects within a global order.

Like celebratory multiculturalism and racial liberalism, this discourse of diaspora development offers minoritarian forms of inclusion within dominant nationalisms and capitalist relations. In this sense, the turn to diasporas for new development actors is the current trajectory of global capitalism, particularly in U.S.-dominated agencies and the postwar rise of neoliberalism. The rearticulation of migrant subjects from "immigrant" to "diasporic" is not necessarily a move away from the nation-state as the primary unit of analysis and toward the acknowledgment of the transnational scope of migrants' lives but rather the resubjectivization of their roles for national development under globalization.

This book forgoes policy-oriented evaluations that measure the impact that diasporic investments, remittances, and philanthropy have or potentially have on homeland states; instead, the cultural analytics it employs disrupt the dominance of development-related categories such as "impact," "best practices," and "efficiency" as transparent metrics of diaspora-homeland relations. Neoliberalism redefines diaspora and homeland in relation to the market, creating "new forms of inclusion, setting apart some citizen-subjects, and creating new spaces" in diaspora and homeland development.[44] Diaspora development discourse contributes to a political economic moment infused with logics that promote efficiency, privatization, and commodification, not only as a matter of state policy but also in everyday transnational lives.

While multilateral and international bodies work to harness diaspora-driven development from above, Filipino Americans do not necessarily accept development's dictates in how they give back or draw meaning from their giving practices. I am primarily concerned with how Filipino American giving practices stand in opposition to neoliberal market logics and the dehistoricization of poverty. Giving back in the context of Filipino America expresses the bonds of diaspora, ties that bind, which could undergird the hierarchies of development or challenge those terms of belonging. The complexity and contingencies of philanthropy and charity, however, are lost in the congratulatory celebration of giving back and their normalization in global capitalist economies.

Many critics note that charity and philanthropy perpetuate inequalities that are produced in capitalistic relations, which is compounded by the undertheorization of the nonprofit sector in critiques of capitalism. Drawing on Marx and Engels's condemnation of bourgeois society, Joan Roelofs argues that the nonprofit sector enables capitalism: "Those who wish to promote change should look closely at what sustains the present system. One reason capitalism doesn't collapse despite its many weaknesses and valiant opposition movements is because of the 'nonprofit sector.' Yet philanthropic capital, its investment and its distribution, are generally neglected by the critics of capitalism."[45] Quoting Marx and Engels, Roelofs claims that researchers have largely failed to address their points in the context of charity and philanthropy, the relations of production, and the way that sectors of the bourgeoisie are "desirous of redressing social grievances, in order to secure the continued existence of bourgeois society."[46] Safeguarding bourgeois society, philanthropy and charity guide the missions of formal organizations that deliver services or execute other programs for those in need, and, as social and cultural institutions, they promulgate dominant perceptions of society and social change. This captures the history of modern philanthropy in the United States, which originally sprang from the need of monopoly capitalists to protect their wealth.

In the first half of the twentieth century, John D. Rockefeller Sr. created his world-renowned, eponymous foundation in response to fears of the power of flourishing monopolies. In other words, the moral force and social reformism of progressivism also manufactured a system for mitigating social ills through "the application of rational social planning and scientific expertise" that provided legitimacy and purpose to these foundations.[47] As foundation head, Rockefeller created philanthropic programs that funded research and contributed to policies that would continue to shape society according to the needs of rampant capitalist accumulation.[48] Philanthropic foundations thus epitomize largely unregulated concentrations of power that help maintain a global political and economic order, encouraging considerations of who or what philanthropy ultimately serves.[49]

Most Filipino Americans would not see their small-scale giving practices as part of the same conversation as corporate foundations or billionaire benefactors. However, values related to giving and assumptions of the unadulterated good of giving are deeply woven into the fabric of American culture and society. As seen in Beveridge, appeals to charity in the Philippines operate in the interpellation of national subjects on both sides of the Pacific. Giving in the contemporary Filipino American diaspora must be understood along with the nonprofit sector's ability to conceal social injustice and operate as both complement and supplement to capitalism, betraying communitarian claims of the "nonprofit" as if it were singularly devoid of the violence of profit-driven institutions.[50]

I understand giving back in terms of frameworks for imagining social transformation and Philippine futures, inseparable from genealogies and political economies of charity, philanthropy, and development. In *Fantasy-Production*, Neferti Tadiar argues, "Imagination, as culturally organized social practice, is an intrinsic, constitutive part of political economy."[51] For Tadiar, fantasy-production denotes "the imaginary of a regime of accumulation and representation of universal value, under the sway of which capitalist nations organize themselves individually and collectively in the 'system' of the Free World." She explains:

> The dreams of Filipinos, rulers and ruled, cannot be understood apart from the global material imaginary, this dominant field of reality, on which they play out. To cast these dreams as the expressions of autonomous, self-contained Filipino subjects (whether they aspire to or resist world power) is to ignore the global order of dreamwork in which the international media system, the source of many of our interpretative representations of the world, plays a constitutive and paradigmatic role.[52]

Some in nonprofit studies situate charity and philanthropy at opposite poles, "the one concrete and individual, the other abstract and institutional."[53] However, in aligning charity with concrete and individual practice, nonprofit studies contribute to the "ongoing pattern of denial" of American empire across the disciplines.[54] That is, such studies ignore the cultural and political work of charitable discourse in national and imperial formations, subjectivization, and the dreamwork of the global order. Reading Beveridge's example through Tadiar's conceptual analysis, the telos of charity as civilizing mission can be understood as "the reconciliation of the individual with the social order."[55] Charity, philanthropy, and development are foundational to international and global dreamwork.

Giving Back intervenes in the reification of diasporic homeland benevolence and altruism, arguing that homeland giving practices both regulate and produce alternative Filipino American and diasporic subjects and formations. At the same time, charity, philanthropy, and development from the United States to the Philippines or from the Filipino American diaspora to the homeland do not operate solely from positions of unilateral power. Cultural studies theorizations of diaspora underscore the multidirectionality, materiality, and economics of diaspora that revise many of the assumptions of development, what it means to help, and what is gained in the processes, practices, and institutions of giving "situated against a backdrop of the global economy of giving" established in colonial, development, and philanthropic relations.[56]

Diaspora Giving

Late modernity shapes contemporary giving practices, which nonetheless bear the material histories of colonialism, monopoly capitalist philanthropy, and official development, which in turn are infused with neoliberal emphases on personal responsibility, the privatization of social welfare, and market solutions to problems of injustice. Geographer Gillian Hart usefully differentiates official development or "big D" development from nonofficial or "small d" development, referring to the "small d" "development of capitalism as geographically uneven, [a] profoundly contradictory set of historical processes."[57] "The moral concern for Filipino society," writes Tadiar, "translates into an economic concern for its competitive advancement," an economism that structures definitions of poverty and solutions for eradicating macrolevel suffering.[58] Developmentalist and extractive market logics compel states and subjects to integrate into the global economy through the ethics and social relations of charity, philanthropy, and development.

The founders and leaders of Filipino American organizations I interview and whose writings I analyze bear little resemblance to the clamor of a pro-imperialist politician rallying the American public over a century ago. Previously quoted organizational leaders Lydia Tanguilig and Geraldine Bigay, in their respective use of "charity begins at home," do not offer pleas for national unity through military and economic control of the Philippines and the colonial uplift of the Filipino people but instead evidence a keen awareness of the obligations of giving back structured by Philippine and Filipino American nationalisms. In their own ways, both display a desire to create relationships of giving, home, and belonging to counter dominant nationalisms and migrant economies; both comment on their own efforts to work with or assist communities in the Philippines as interventions in Filipinoness. Despite the forces that structure giving-related institutions in global capitalism, Filipino Americans envision giving practices and imagine Philippine futures that work within, alongside, and against the hegemony of charity, philanthropy, development, and the imperialist divisions of global space.

Shifting the object of research from development or philanthropy to diaspora giving, I examine the operations of neoliberalism and the aftermath of American empire in transnational diaspora formation. Diaspora giving endeavors to resituate questions of love (love for the homeland and the etymological roots of philanthropy, which refers to the love of humanity), homeland and home, and obligation (to families, communities, the poor, the nation) in the economies and logics of global capital. Diaspora giving and these issues of love, home, and obligation exist simultaneously with the global capitalist reproduction of poverty and U.S. militarism in the Philippines. They exist simultaneously with the racialized exploitation of Filipino laborers in international labor markets and the racialized order of the United States. Diaspora giving encompasses forces of subjection as well as alternative ways of imagining diasporic returns and Philippine futures from afar. Discursively, diaspora giving figures in broad markers of cultural authenticity for Filipinos in how giving so frequently measures Filipinoness in diaspora. Hierarchies emerge between diaspora and homeland and between Filipino America and the Philippines in how the giver draws authority (or is given authority) through cultural values placed on American citizenship and mobility, an ironic legacy of Senator Beveridge and his ilk.

The rapidity in the increase of migration spurred by late capitalism coincides with shifts in the humanitarian imagination. Just as rates and networks of migration have created new diasporas of mobile populations whose movements are guided by the transformations of global capital and production, such as the generalized shift in the United States away from intensive industrial production to service- and finance-oriented economies, a reconfiguration in the public discourse of humanitarian crises has also occurred. An "international moral discourse" supported by the international media that connects local efforts to systems of international NGOs now influences how everyday people—those whose jobs or training are not primarily in NGO program management or development research—respond to humanitarian crises.[59] Practices and processes related to Filipino American diaspora giving tell a part of this multifaceted story, at the very least for the zeal with which the Philippine state, development agencies, news media, nonprofit organizations, NGOs, and Filipino Americans have all taken up the language of diaspora development and diaspora philanthropy.

I read giving, including remittance giving, as comprising forms of diasporic return. In this sense, my work is a companion to Eric J. Pido's book on real estate "returns," which Filipino Americans make when buying land and property in the Philippines for their retirement years, as a growing strategy of Philippine development.[60] In terms of monetary diasporic returns to the Philippines, overseas Filipinos send more money from the United States to family in the Philippines than from any other country. In terms of location, over one-third of all overseas Filipinos are in the United States, and they initiate the vast majority of philanthropic projects and medical missions to the Philippines.[61] This book does not use these statistics alone to speak to the analytical purchase of Filipino American diaspora giving. Rather, it begins with the premise that diaspora development in the Global South is enacted and imagined through negotiations with and in relation to the Global North, especially given the neocolonial alliance between the Philippines and the United States. The exceptionalism of American empire was made through its professed commitment to benevolence; that official development in the third world was integral to U.S. cold war strategies to ensure its spread of democratic capitalism; and that philanthropy is as complementary to global capitalism today as it was to monopoly capitalism. These premises inform my critique of the power and meaning of giving back.

Nermeen Shaikh addresses the cultural work of America's exceptionalism that mediates the contradictions of colonialism, development, and capitalism: "It must be assumed that the U.S. is always acting with good intentions, and if events unfold in such a way as to suggest otherwise, then each instance is simply a betrayal of the original intent, which is itself beyond reproach or at the very least, absolved of the worst offences."[62] "Who," Shaikh asks, "after all, can apprehend the world, the idea of humanity, as a whole? What enables such a perspective? Who can desire to change that 'world'?"[63] Good intentions aside, historical and material conditions dictate who is and who is not allowed or encouraged to apprehend solutions to poverty or to intervene in social suffering. This book brings to light these perspectives and desires, as well as their mutability—how such perspectives and desires, such as benevolence and American exceptionalism, are transformed and mediated in migration, immigration, and diaspora.

Diaspora giving provides a lens through which to read my archive, allowing an examination of the simultaneities of unity and hierarchy, discourse and practice, the global and deeply personal, mobility and rootedness, home and abroad. Inserting Filipino Americans and the Philippines into this conversation expands not only a reflection on the forms of philanthropy that are practiced by Filipino Americans. An examination of Filipino Americans and the Philippines requires a consideration of the systemic causes of migration from the Philippines and to the United States, the structure of desires for homeland return, the economic stagnation of the Philippines, and the global maintenance of gross inequality. In this context, neocolonialism, developmentalism, and neoliberal global capitalism have normalized philanthropy as the solution to social problems: problems that neocolonialism, structural adjustment and the repayment of third-world debt, the privatization of social welfare and dismantling of the welfare state, the normalization of corporate interests in social relations, and the violence endemic to global capitalism created, reproduce, and exacerbate. Critical scholars in transnational feminist studies, queer studies, and Asian American cultural studies cogently illustrate how power operates in the diasporic contexts of global capitalism, and my work contributes to this conversation, highlighting the developmentalist logics that pervade the discourse of giving back and its links to Filipinoness. Diaspora giving highlights the forces and processes that attempt to stabilize homeland and Filipinoness as well as the developmentalist logics of globalization—in and *in the name of* diaspora. This project suggests that sanctioned forms of giving back contain or circumscribe other forms of transnational responsibility, obligation, and mobility and alternative imaginings and modes of homeland return. It elaborates on the cultural elements, the socialities that are produced, and the broader implications of giving back.

This project was inspired in part by Isagani Sarmiento's 2002 self-published book, *Re-building the Roots of a Nation.*[64] A founder and president of a Filipino American NGO with the goal of uniting Filipino Americans in a fight against poverty in the Philippines, Sarmiento argues there can be no economic or social development in the Philippines without first addressing cultural traits of Filipinos in the Philippines. Sarmiento conveys his purview through a curious expression: "If you live in a garlic house all your life, you will smell like garlic and not know it."[65] The garlic house symbolizes that which prevents the Philippines from being an economically viable and independent nation. "Is the Philippines a 'garlic house,' or is the 'garlic house' within the Filipino?" he asks.[66] Having left the Philippines to work in the United States, Sarmiento narrates himself as having escaped the damaging Philippine culture. His migration produced the ability to identify the problems of Filipinos and to help others out of their own garlic houses and out of poverty. His motivation for giving back is to teach other Filipinos that they too can learn how to do this for themselves:

> Come! Let us all come out of our garlic houses, and when we are already outside [them], let us then reason together! Join me in coming out of our cages. There is our country, the Philippines, who is waiting for us to serve her. Our country needs

> help to extricate our nation from its economic and political mud hole. Only those outside the "garlic house," those who are free and independent from their cages, possess the privilege of recognizing, knowing and dealing with the "garlic" taste and smell. Let us help each other to find the right reason. Let us derive more meaning and purpose for what we do. . . . I no longer possess the wings of a caged bird, but the wings that can fly in the sky, as high as I want. From above my cage, I could see the many harmful paradigms that shaped my psyche, those that virtually caged me from being free within.[67]

Sarmiento wants to help Filipinos in the Philippines recognize their flaws. He imagines a Filipino diaspora that is unified through service to this desire. However, the culture-of-poverty thesis of the garlic house fails to examine the concentration of land and political and economic control in the Philippines in a small handful of families or the reproduction of inequality in global capitalist relations. Sarmiento's observations demonstrate that the "roots of the nation" produce morally differentiated spaces, developmentally arranged according to a framework of social transformation that has long shaped the hope for Philippine futures.

The context of contemporary Filipino American diaspora giving must be understood through American imperialism and genealogies of benevolence and development, global capitalism, the politics of immigration and migration, and dominant spatial and subject formations. *Giving Back* asks questions such as these: In what ways does giving from Filipino America articulate home (and the multiplicity of homes and homeland), duty, and benevolence in diaspora formation? Given neocolonial relations that extract labor from the Philippines in new ways for the global market, how do Filipino Americans—in relationship to Filipinos in the Philippines as well as to Filipino contract laborers in countries in the Middle East, Asia, and Europe—mobilize their American cultural citizenship to authorize their social-development projects in the Philippines and thus their ability to return to the homeland? Relatedly, how does the Philippine state construct differentiated diaspora-giving subjects who are amenable to American exceptionalism?

Diaspora giving points to how the space of diaspora, its emotional resonance, its role in globalized economies, and its borders are produced in and through various Filipino American transnational efforts to improve the conditions and futures of the Philippine homeland. I use the attributional noun "diaspora" rather than the adjectival "diasporic" in "diaspora giving" to privilege a deliberation on the multiplicity of giving practices, identities, and subjectivities in processes of diaspora formation. In a similar vein, this work employs the verbal noun "giving" (and not the noun "gifts") to address the complex cultural politics that arise when organizations position themselves as not only the voice of the Filipino American community but also as authorities on social development in the Philippines. To give speaks not only to a gift that is given but also to the relationships and divisions between giver and receiver and the social, political, ethical, and economic contexts of those relationships and divisions. How Filipino American organizations negotiate those contexts and relationships tells us something about contemporary diaspora formation and discourses of Filipinoness. To give also speaks to a yielding, a giving way of a position or a force that may have at one time been seen as natural or impenetrable. Diaspora-giving critique points to the contestations of hegemonic giving institutions and logics. It marks alternative imaginaries of social transformation that disrupt normative geographies of the Global North and the Global South from the space of diaspora.

A motivating concern of this book is how giving back can stabilize overlapping systems of inequality. In this, I draw on scholars in philanthropy, nonprofit, and foundation studies such as Patricia Mooney Nickel and Angela Eikenberry, who show how the current market-based discourse of philanthropy depoliticizes the negative effects of the market that marketized philanthropy then seeks to rectify.[68] Nickel and Eikenberry work to subject marketized philanthropy—and everything that this philanthropic practice seeks to transform in society—to a discourse about its meaning, arguing that "in order for philanthropy to instigate a transformative discourse aimed at improving everyday life, it must stand apart from the systemic causes of poverty—namely, the market and the neoliberal state."[69] All Filipino Americans who commit their time and resources to giving back express a desire for transformation. I examine diaspora giving to work against not only the marketization of philanthropic relationships but also the subordination of diasporic relationships to the market and development, which confine the nature of transformation.

The chapters work together to delineate and thematize the multiple and contradictory approaches to giving back as a discourse of diasporic belonging. Chapter 1 draws attention to the Philippines as a neocolonial state, with implications for Filipino migration and for the structures that guide remittances and philanthropy from Filipinos back to the Philippines. When the state empowers its citizens to work abroad and celebrates the remittances and philanthropic returns from migrants and immigrants, it deflects attention regarding the state's responsibility in addressing the material conditions of poverty and need. Chapter 2 historicizes the diasporic turn to social development and philanthropy as a respite from the messiness of politics. As a result of this faith in social development, social and collective issues are depoliticized, and so is the homeland orientation of diaspora. Chapter 3 works to understand the contradictions of corporate social-responsibility programs in diaspora, drawing attention to the tragically close relationship between giving to assuage or remedy social needs and profiting from the production of need. Corporate foundations and state development push diaspora toward certain approaches to giving back over others. Chapter 4 reflects on the challenges in navigating diaspora giving with a purposeful and critical sense of responsibility that takes account of the differences, places, and relationships produced by the Philippines' remittance economy, the global recruitment of racialized and gendered Filipino care workers, the antipolitics of social development, and the neoliberal erasure of the roots of poverty.

Overview of the Book

Chapter 1 connects the frameworks presented in this Introduction to an analysis of American dream ideology in Filipino diaspora giving. The "charitable gift" of American democratic institutions marked the difference between American colonialism in the Pacific and older European empires, and the country's dreams of exceptionalism rested on the subjectivization of the Filipino colonial body. In more recent decades, American dream ideology incorporates Filipino subjects through moral figurations of migration and homeland returns. Emphasizing the plural form of homeland *returns* rather than a singular and definitive homeland return, I attend to the social and cultural values placed on the economic *returns* of migration, which I interpret as giving back to the homeland through philanthropy, social development, and remittances. The chapter demonstrates that expectations for non-U.S.-based Filipino migrants differ considerably from those of Filipino American immigrants. It shows that overseas Filipino labor migrants are required by both the Philippine state and national culture to provide economic remittance returns, while Filipino Americans are celebrated for their voluntary philanthropic efforts. By making remittance returns, philanthropic returns, and volunteer returns to the homeland an obligation of diasporic belonging, the Philippine state asserts that social needs can be remedied from the diaspora. In my analysis, I challenge normative valuations of overseas Filipino migrant laborers and Filipino Americans through an extended examination of homeland returns. I argue that these two figures of Filipino migration and mobility are mutually constituted and deployed through discourses, institutions, and practices of "doing good"—a dominant formation that relies on norms and relationships of beneficence, morality, and sacrifice.

Chapter 2 proposes a countercritique that actively attends to the political consequences of migration for diaspora. A consequence of contemporary migration is that political and social commitments are channeled primarily to the homeland and not toward the Filipino American's home in the United States. Filipino Americans are conditioned to split their diasporic practice from the transnational forces that tie the United States to the Philippines, Filipinos in the United States to Filipinos elsewhere in the diaspora, and Filipinos in the United States to other racialized and exploited peoples in the places where they live. U.S.-based Filipina novelist, journalist, activist, and organizer Ninotchka Rosca refers to this phenomenon as the bifurcation of transnational lives, and this chapter utilizes her commentary as a springboard to develop a critique of dominant homeland orientation for Filipino American diaspora giving. The chapter turns to the history of martial law in the Marcos-era Philippines to contextualize Filipino American homeland orientation since the 1970s and discusses how a dominant Filipino American homeland orientation, given meaning through its antipolitics, emerged immediately after the fall of Ferdinand Marcos. I analyze how Rosca's political discourse disorients dominant homeland orientation and the force of developmentalism.

Chapter 3 deconstructs a dominant discourse of poverty in Filipino American diaspora giving: the normalization of market solutions to poverty and inequality. To display the limits of developmentalist discourse introduced in dominant diaspora-giving frameworks of social transformation in Chapter 2, I read the self-representation of the Ayala Foundation and the Ayala Foundation USA (now called Philippine Development Foundation) and their significant contributions to shaping Filipino American diaspora philanthropy. I contend that the diaspora giving promoted by these foundations consolidates this dominant discourse of poverty with a corporate sense of responsibility. I point to Ayala's dominance in the Philippine economy, bringing attention to the role corporate conglomerates play in the creation of poverty, to indicate how the discourse on poverty engaged by Ayala Foundation USA cannot account for the rich getting so much richer in neoliberal capitalism. Chapter 3 contextualizes the ideological work performed by the corporate foundations and considers the material implications of their ideals and practices regarding the politics of Filipino American diaspora giving.

Chapter 4 offers another example of counterhegemonic diaspora-giving practice. I analyze the Philippine environment to guide the critique toward a transnational ecological mindedness that connects the urgency of responses compelled by environmental disaster to diasporic frameworks of social transformation that account for the production of third-world vulnerability and the reproduction of poverty in global capital. In this homeland reorientation, one would account for the genealogy of developmentalism in the Philippines and chart responsibility that stems from the hierarchies of global capitalism. The first part of the chapter considers a tendency to narrate the environmental space of the Philippines through its beauty and the consequence of this tendency for diaspora giving. The chapter then turns to an examination of the Filipino/American Coalition for Environmental Solidarity (FACES), a U.S.-based environmental-justice organization originally founded to bring attention and reparations to the environmental devastation wrought by the former U.S. military bases in the Philippines. I argue that FACES disorients dominant diaspora-giving practices by connecting environmental issues in the Philippines to environmental issues in the United States and elsewhere. FACES imagines counterhegemonic ways of giving that address the inequalities that diaspora giving, in the abstract, purportedly sets itself to combat.

The Epilogue is a brief rumination on the messiness of diasporic return and the affective forces that drive Filipino Americans toward action. "Love" serves as a mantra for many diaspora-giving organizations and projects, but this idea of love requires that critical attention be paid to how such complex expressions of loyalty, intimacy, and attachment translate in the institutionalization and practice of diaspora giving. I end the book by narrating how the idea for this project began. I turn to its origin story, so to speak, to show that diaspora giving, for me, has always been about the dreams, limitations, and ineffability of love.

1

Good Diasporic Returns

Immigrant Philanthropy, Overseas Labor Remittances, and the American Dream

Filipinos want to partake of "the American Dream," when in fact they are already a constitutive part of that dream.

—Neferti Xina M. Tadiar, *Fantasy-Production*

The epigraph here confronts the puzzlement of the American dream. Filipinos, while desirous of the perceived benefits of America, have helped bring this ideology into existence—but from outside its imagined borders, as flawed objects of comparison and as its conditional beneficiaries. Good Filipino subjects, whether in the Philippines, in the United States, in the Middle East, or in transit, have always been a constitutive part of the American dream. The instrumental versatility of Filipinos to the American dream can be tracked from early twentieth-century colonial benevolence in the Philippines to the Asian American model-minority myth and its geopolitical cold war origins and from neoliberal logics of more recent decades that underlie a culture of global Filipino migration. As colonial subjects in the early twentieth century, cast as ready to be remade in the image of America and its democratic traditions and institutions, Filipinos facilitated the American dream of territorial and global market expansion.[1] Representations of middle-class Filipino Americans, and others who were deemed model minorities, as professional immigrants to the United States, celebrated for their economic assimilation, helped uphold the American dream of meritocracy for a public that continues to discipline poor people of color.[2]

Certain organized efforts against restrictive immigration and racist deportation policies reflect the ways in which American dream ideology perpetuates the binary and comparative valuation of desirable/undesirable migrants and would-be migrants.[3] These efforts, at their core, function as safeguards for hegemonic whiteness.

The twenty-first century presents another avenue for the conscription of Filipinos in the reproduction of the American dream. Economic globalization produces new occasions for Filipinos to serve Western economic interests and U.S. investments as a primary global power. As in the colonial moment, good Filipino subjects accept the terms of service to the interests and promises of America, as migrants not only to the United States but from the Philippines as a former U.S. territory. Unlike what occurred in the colonial moment, Filipinos now serve these interests from the United States, the Philippines, and beyond. For example, in 2004 former Philippine secretary of labor and employment and current chairperson of the Development Bank of the Philippines, Patricia A. Santo Tomas, told a reporter, "Our traits as a people lend ourselves well to being part of the [global] service industry. . . . Perhaps that is what globalization means to us."[4] Santo Tomas integrates a national identity with the global economy in her description. She also suggests that Filipinos are a constitutive part of the American dream today in their service as migrant subjects, a critical examination of which, to borrow a phrasing from Filipino studies cultural theorist Lucy Mae San Pablo Burns, "makes transparent the continuing *reconstitution* of the U.S.-Philippine imperial relations."[5] In emphasizing how Filipinos "lend [them]selves well" to the global labor market, Santo Tomas marks the terms by which gendered and racialized Filipino migrant workers make measurable contributions to the Philippines, becoming good Filipino subjects through their mobility and migration.

In contradistinction to this transnational "contributionism," Neferti Xina M. Tadiar and Dylan Rodríguez, among others, attend to the consequences of the American dream and the terms of valuation that enable or supplement white supremacy and the transnational exploitation of labor.[6] Diaspora giving is tied to the language of mobility, and this analysis suggests we pay attention to the transnational and transhistorical dimensions of the American dream, of what it means to participate in and historically mark a social imagining integral to the legitimation of Filipinos' role in globalization and the returns on their labor and migration. Signifying practices of giving-related organizations and institutions illustrate diaspora space as a kind of contact zone, Mary Louise Pratt's invocation of imperial encounters, of "the space and time where subjects previously separated by geography and history are co-present, the point at which their trajectories now intersect."[7]

This chapter extends the established scholarship on Filipino migration and diaspora and works to understand how the American dream and the global order, to which Santo Tomas seems both resigned and committed, serve as the grounds on which contemporary figures of Filipino mobility are constituted. I look to the figure of Filipino migration most associated with the American dream, the Filipino American immigrant, in relationship to the figure circulated in the discourse on the global service economy, the overseas Filipino labor migrant. I examine the Filipino American immigrant and the overseas Filipino labor migrant as mutually constituted figures of migration, mobility, and return, even when imagined as apparent opposites and in tension with one another in their access to doing good.

I first examine the dominant discourses surrounding ideas of "doing good" in diaspora. I show the varied relationships that diasporic figures have with the Philippines to uncover the relational ideological positioning of Filipino Americans and overseas Filipino labor migrants.[8] I link this to my exploration of the American dream to illustrate the cultural work that is carried by promises of the good life in the United States. These fantasies situate overseas labor migrants as aspirational subjects whose giving is both required and suspect and Filipino American immigrants as subjects whose giving is proof of their well-deserved cultural citizenship in the United States. I challenge normative valuations of mobile Filipino subjects through an extended examination of returns in awards programs for Filipino migrants and immigrants of the Philippine state and personal interviews with Filipino American presidents and founders of diasporic philanthropic organizations to reveal the stakes of nationalist and identitarian forms of collective identity. Reading the chapter's archive through the lens of doing good highlights the hegemony of beneficent homeland returns and the ways that diasporic discourse can operate to contain the excesses of migration, ensuring that the Philippines remains a labor-sending country for the global service industry and augmenting the idealization of America and the global order.

"Good News for the Poor"

In 2006 Jeremaiah Opiniano, the widely respected director of the Institute for Migration and Development Issues in the Philippines, organized a conference on what he and others call "diaspora philanthropy." "For philanthropy experts," states Opiniano in the conference literature, "people are beginning to find out how Filipino migrants can be tapped [for] . . . development purposes in the homeland."[9] The conference, held at the University of Santo Tomas in Manila, convened many experts who were interested in sharing best practices for channeling resources from Filipino migrants and immigrants toward social development and philanthropic purposes in the Philippines. The event brought representatives from Filipino organizations based in Japan, Singapore, and, chiefly, the United States together with those from overseas migrant worker advocacy organizations, corporate foundations, and government bodies in the Philippines related to the oversight of migration, remittances from overseas migrant workers, and philanthropy from Filipinos living abroad. Per Opiniano, the conference acknowledged the collective efforts of Filipinos, stating that no matter where Filipinos live, no matter if one works as an executive director of a corporate foundation or creates ways to help the homeland on top of life's daily obligations, "we" all just want change for the Philippines. This rhetorical "we" signifies a unified Filipino identity and holds it to a moral standard. Filipino immigrants and migrants of different class status and regional affiliation are not united simply through blood, dispersion from the homeland, or cultural norms and practices but also through action toward a greater good, a beneficent homeland return.

Giving back to the homeland with some level of attention to the overall betterment of the country is the fundamental value in this diasporic ideal. As occurs for all ideals, ties that bind come up against the lived and affective realities of diasporic experience. Within the opening plenary, the tensions of the conference's model of unified Filipino diaspora made themselves known. The conference, titled

"Good News for the Poor: A Conference on Filipino Diaspora Philanthropy," could not contain the differences related to the contexts and consequences of migration. During the question-and-answer session following the opening address, a woman, who I later found out works for a migrant labor advocacy organization in the Philippines, challenged the premise of the conference itself. She began, "I am very concerned with the name, 'Good News for the Poor.' Why is this so much 'good news'?" With palpable anxiety, the woman stated that 90 percent of what she hears from her organization is about problems with migrant workers and their families in the Philippines, problems of fidelity, incest, indolence, and abuse: "What can NGOs and the government do to help the families, especially those left behind?" This conference attendee appealed to NGOs and government agents to "take the side of those harmed by globalization," a precondition of diaspora philanthropy that calls into question the migrant laborer's willingness to accept the consequences of labor migration and the terms of one's sacrifice.[10] This sacrifice, the speaker implies, is problematically gendered as the "harms" she identifies that correlate to normative notions of the family, marriage, masculinity, and femininity. Additionally, her critique draws attention to one of the most ubiquitous pitfalls of philanthropy as a social and cultural institution—the paternalism of the giving subject with the agency to identify the best solution to poverty on behalf of the poor. The speaker, displeased with the assumptions of good news, highlights the multiple moving parts between the goodness of giving back and the underbelly of international labor migration and, in so doing, renarrates conventional histories of Filipino migration and return. In global capitalism, Filipinos enter history or become historical agents as willing global labor migrants, a logic that was most vehemently rejected by this speaker.

This example serves as an entry point for important reflections on doing good as its own institution in the production and cultural work of diaspora in which the projected image of their communion as Filipino and motivations for homeland return pivot on a larger sense of responsibility and moral commitment.[11] Doing good in diaspora is never simply self-evident; it is channeled by the material, affective, and cultural forces that bring about its conditions. In this chapter, I use the term "doing good"—philanthropic initiatives, related discourses and collective practices of generosity, obligation, and the context of their institutionalization—as an interpretive framework for understanding the processes of Filipino diaspora formation animated by linked moral figurations of migration and returns.

Premised on this logic, the "Good News for the Poor" conference semiotically separates the poor Filipino, the object of beneficence, from the diasporic Filipino philanthropist. In practice, these traits are never simply discrete; the persons giving back may be poor, or perhaps recipients may not see philanthropy as good news given the realities of their lives or the choices that they would make for themselves. Moreover, it was clear to the aforementioned speaker that the conference failed to capture how she understood the relationship between doing good and the negative consequences of labor migration. Not only did the conference attendee question the framework of "good news for the poor," which itself is a challenge to the purity of benevolence and the fundamental morality of giving, but she demanded that a celebration of Filipino diasporic unity be tempered. She understood neoliberal globalization as responsible for the ramifications of migration—incest, indolence, and abuse (not "good news")—that qualify doing good in diaspora, rejecting the norms of diaspora philanthropy that would serve to distinguish ideal Filipinos from its excess. "Good news" both "manages and disavows the contradictions of a world economic system built and sustained by racialized and gendered violence and exploitation, on the one hand, and free market capitalism as the symbolic epitome of racial and gendered equality, on the other."[12] Thus, when this advocate for migrant workers, a former migrant worker herself, disrupts the premise of the conference, she makes a trenchant critique of global capital.

At this conference, which included participants from Philippine agencies and Filipino organizations from at least a half-dozen countries, the Filipino American immigrant emerged as the implied benevolent subject, thus echoing developmentalist narratives of subjectivity in the historical reconstitution of U.S.-Philippine relations. The conference workshops highlighted presentations from Filipino American organizations, and Filipino American representatives spoke as experts on envisioning and monitoring philanthropic and social-development projects in the Philippines. The workshops positioned Filipino American organizational leaders as model diasporans, a phenomenon that extends to national discourses of migration and return. For example, one workshop was led by the founder of the San Francisco organization Save a Tahanan, a champion of microfinance in the Philippines that uses the tagline "Providing opportunity is our moral obligation."[13] Another workshop was organized by a representative of Feed the Hungry, Inc. of the greater Washington, D.C., area, which describes its programs in the Philippines and organizational mission this way: "To uplift the spirit and well-being of the poorest of the poor, the abused and the desolate through gift giving, livelihood, nutritional and educational programs, classroom and housing projects, and natural disaster and medical assistance."[14] The emotional outburst shows not only the outer bounds of the legitimacy of the state discourse of globalization and the state-directed export of racialized and gendered bodies but also the obverse of these Filipino American organizations' claims about the morality of giving.

I do not intend to besmirch the intentions of Filipino Americans and their organizations or claim that they are lackeys of global capital. Rather, I believe that doing good is a temporally and spatially contingent discourse in which the perceived benefits of globalization and of diaspora are associated with American exceptionalism. The consequences of labor migration described previously and the contradictions of globalization and American imperialism highlight the necessity of naming the conditions of doing good through the processes of valuation and devaluation of one population in relationship to another. The Filipino American immigrant and the overseas Filipino labor migrant are taken up here to read their difference deployed through discourses, institutions, and practices of doing good—a dominant epistemological formation of Filipino diaspora and a neoliberal apparatus that relies on norms and relationships of beneficence, morality, and sacrifice.

Only 3 percent of overseas Filipino workers—migrants working on contract and maintaining Philippine citizenship—live in the United States, while 65 percent of Filipino permanent residents or expatriates live in the United States.[15] Differences certainly exist between the groups, particularly in terms of permanent residency in the country where one works (this status is denied to most contract laborers), one's right to state protection as a permanent resident or naturalized citizen, and the political and social capital that these differences engender. Stark divisions and hierarchies exist within each category, but I am more concerned with how the Filipino American immigrant and the overseas Filipino labor migrant are social categories of valuation that link Filipinoness to the terms and conditions of doing good in diaspora. Like Denise Cruz's delineation of the "transpacific Filipina" in moments of imperial transition, reading the Filipino American immigrant and the overseas Filipino labor migrant as mutually constituted figures of representation reveals that, together, they are "crucial to national definition, to identities and communities at home and abroad, and to the reformation of the Philippines' changing interactions with other nations."[16]

Khachig Tölölyan, among others, departs from classical understandings of diaspora and diasporic hopes to one day return to the homeland en masse. Instead of a literal return in fulfillment of a diasporan's destiny of return, Tölölyan emphasizes "'re-turn' without actual repatriation: that is, they turn again and again toward the homeland through travel, remittances, cultural exchange, and political lobbying and by various contingent efforts to maintain other links with the homeland."[17] The desire to unify migrant populations as a strategy for homeland development is not unique to the "Good News for the Poor" conference or to Filipinos. Rather, the increased privatization of social needs worldwide aligns with a global project propelled by state bodies and multilateral organizations to interpellate diasporans as the new development agents of the twenty-first century, contributing to the stakes of such calls for diasporic unification.

Calls for diasporic unity through giving activities are continually made by a wide variety of organizations, but scholars, the Philippine government, and the news media still differentiate between the Filipino American immigrant and the overseas Filipino labor migrant on the basis of class and formal citizenship status. In naming the categories and assigning meaning according to status as Filipino American immigrant or overseas Filipino labor migrant, experts on Filipino migration, including Filomeno Aguilar, chart differences that carry implications for the reception of immigrants and migrants within national culture. Aguilar reifies these purported differences between the "merely symbolic" ethnicity of Filipino immigrants and the Filipino labor migrant's indisputable national identity. This idealized mode of comparison renders invisible their mutual constitution and relational valuation:

> Unlike immigrants, most labor migrants on fixed-term contracts are not granted permanent resident status, and thus prevented from identification with and sociopolitical incorporation to the labor-receiving states. Immigrants in one context may disregard Filipinoness but revive it on certain occasions, or in other contexts uphold it as a basis of difference; labor migrants, for their part, cannot hang on to their national identity in a merely symbolic way.[18]

In a slight to the authenticity, as it were, of Filipino immigrants (the majority of whom are in the United States), Aguilar's emphasis on whether Filipino immigrants choose to orient toward the homeland extends assimilationist discourse, lending power to the terms of racial inclusion within liberal multiculturalism. Doubt is cast on the veracity of an immigrant's Filipinoness and claims of belonging to the Philippine homeland; Aguilar's figures of Filipinoness fail to capture the nuances and diversity of sociality, experience, and emotional lives, which Filipino studies scholars theorize in terms of ambivalence and competing pulls of responsibility and identification. Anthropologist Benito M. Vergara helps clarify these processes, expanding Tölölyan's work on diasporic experience and the repeated turning to the concept and/or reality of homeland in everyday life. For Filipinos in the United States, the repeated turning toward the homeland contradicts the logic of assimilation, but more important, according to Vergara, remembrances of and obligations to homeland are "accompanied by a complementary and contradictory turn to their adoptive home even before their arrival."[19] "The *image* of Filipino life in America, as held by Filipinos in the Philippines," Vergara continues, "is a relevant social fact, as it both informs, and is informed by, the actual conditions in the United States."[20] Restrictive settlement policies in Japan, Abu Dhabi, and England, for example, do not present permanent residency as a viable option for overseas contract labor migrants in practice or in the national imagination. Because Filipinos in the United States are much more likely than Filipino migrants elsewhere to permanently settle or to obtain citizenship, "Filipino Americans, then, bear the discursive brunt of being seen as 'less Filipino' or as having 'betrayed' the Philippines."[21]

The cultural and political work of doing good demonstrates how diasporas take shape through transnational discourses of the American dream in unexpected ways. As seen in the "Good News for the Poor" conference, doing good in diaspora secures a privileged place in the homeland for Filipino Americans that is denied to overseas Filipino migrant laborers. Philanthropic returns made by Filipino American immigrants extend from their self-determined enactments of doing good as an expression of their Filipinoness, whereas for the overseas labor migrant, doing good is compelled by the nation-state. The transnational circulation of the American dream structures migration by upholding life in the United States as the "good life." The American dream is a prominent theme (and often a lament) in Filipino studies. I build from this critical work to emphasize processes of valuation in that once the good life in America is achieved, one is seen to do good in diaspora in ways that extend from the immigrant's American cultural citizenship. Those not in the United States, the bulk of whom are labor migrants working on contract in almost every other country in the world, do not have access to a valuation of doing good that is safeguarded through cultural citizenship. For overseas Filipino labor migrants outside the United States, the Philippine nation-state is able to maintain punitive control over the mechanisms and the meaning of doing good, manifest through the cultural and political governance of remittances and sacrifice for the good of national development. Doing good denies admittance to those migrants who are subjected by its operations.

The Diaspora/American Dream

The literature on Filipino labor migration routinely discusses the numbers that capture the Philippines' success as the premier labor exporter in the world: "In all, about 8 million Filipinos—an astounding one tenth of the country's citizens—currently work overseas to support families back home," describes a *Newsweek* article.[22] "On average, 3,400 Filipinos leave daily for work abroad, over a million per year, to join the nearly 10 million Filipinos (out of 90 million) already out of the Philippines, scattered around the world. It is the largest global diaspora of migrant labor next to Mexico, the highest per capita exporter of labor in Southeast Asia," according to postcolonial theorist E. San Juan Jr.[23] On the established Migration Information Source website, migration scholar Maruja M. B. Asis reveals the extent of the country's "culture of migration": "Since the 1970s, the Philippines—a country of about 7,000 islands peopled by diverse ethno-linguistic groups—has supplied all kinds of skilled and low-skilled workers to the world's more developed regions. As of December 2004, an estimated 8.1 million Filipinos—nearly 10 percent of the country's 85 million people—were working and/or residing in close to 200 countries and territories."[24]

The number of Filipinos overseas, which almost always refers in each case to overseas Filipino *migrant labor*, both skilled and unskilled, is quoted at around 10 percent of the population. The Commission on Filipinos Overseas produces these statistics, whose latest figure for the stock estimate of overseas Filipinos is 10,238,614.[25] The statistic does much work—socially, politically, and culturally. Philippine officials tout this number to prove the availability, marketability, and desirability of the Filipino laborer in international rankings. In contradistinction, critics of the Philippine government use this number to denounce the national economic development policy of promoting and facilitating overseas Filipino workers. For example, and to draw again from E. San Juan's previously cited article, "Clearly the Philippine government has earned the distinction of being the most migrant- and remittance-dependent ruling apparatus in the world, mainly by virtue of denying its citizens the right to decent employment at home."[26] Supporters and critics of the Philippine state's policies of labor brokerage diverge concerning the government's responsibility either to facilitate labor migration or to provide jobs in the Philippines, but both groups disguise the fact that this number, the eight to eleven million Filipinos overseas, does not reference only labor migrants. Almost one-half of overseas Filipinos maintain permanent residency or citizenship in countries other than the Philippines, the majority of whom live permanently in the United States.[27]

To date, more than 3.5 million Filipinos live in the United States, the majority of whom are not "irregular migrants" lacking visas or work permits or in the United States by way of visas related to their contract work. In fact, the number of Filipinos overseas includes U.S.-born second-generation Filipino Americans, who may or may not even be aware of the phenomenon of global Filipino contract labor migration. By including all Filipino Americans in this total, these organizations pad the Philippines' prominent standing in global labor-export rankings, which, year after year, places the Philippines in the top ten, if not the top three, countries with the highest rates of out-of-country labor migration. This helps the Philippines aggressively market the availability, quality, and affordability of its citizens to the international business world, thus asserting the excellence of its products. Collapsing Filipino Americans into the eight to eleven million Filipinos overseas also deemphasizes Filipino Americans' remittance power. Because labor migration is both celebrated and used as proof of the failures of national leadership to provide opportunities for its citizens, the Philippines must emphasize remittances and their role in buoying the Philippine economy.[28] Folding Filipinos in the United States and elsewhere into the number of Filipino overseas *laborers* detracts attention from the Philippines' continued dependence on the United States through the figure of the Filipino American.

Chronicling the responses of Filipino nurses working in Libya, Saudi Arabia, Singapore, and the United Kingdom, Anna Guevarra writes, "Regardless of their experiences, they were all working to fulfill one aspiration—to *eventually* make it to the United States."[29] Because of the perceived economic benefits and the social and cultural capital that are granted by life in the United States, many Filipinos imagine the United States as the ideal destination and that "working in the United States is *the* ultimate opportunity."[30] The power of this ideal is not lost on the Philippine state or employment agencies in the Philippines. Labor-sending agencies working with the Philippine government, for example, shower would-be migrants with images of life in the United States and suggestions that working in the United States will lead to economic and cultural gains for migrants and also for their families in the Philippines. Cognizant of the promise and allure of working there, as well as the limited number of U.S. immigrant visas and long waiting periods to secure the relatively few visas that are available, employment agencies in the Philippines strategically promote contract work in other countries, such as Saudi Arabia, as stepping-stones to the United States, maintaining the dream of

America while ensuring a continued stream of labor to these other countries.[31] To recall Santo Tomas's unabashed suggestion, providing labor for the global service industry is the most important contribution that the Philippines and Filipino migrant laborers can make.

Neferti Tadiar ruminates on a puzzling dimension of the intersection between diasporic Filipinoness and discourses of the American dream, which, she says, "began in the late nineteenth century as the dream of empire."[32] The colonization of the Philippines enabled dreams of empire in which attempts to civilize Filipino savages offered material proof of the exceptionalism of the United States and its imperial projects. Later, the United States masked its contradictions of racial liberalism for an international cold war audience in part by following through on its plan to grant Philippine independence and relaxing its anti-Asian immigration laws in the 1950s and 1960s. The Immigration and Naturalization Act of 1965 enabled the flows of Filipino professional immigration to the United States, reinforcing the claim that Filipinos function as a constitutive part of the American dream and its universalized promises of middle-class, consumerist life. Professional Filipino Americans became proof that the American dream—and economic assimilation despite racial-minority status—was available for all. Earlier I claim that Filipinos' role in reconstituting the American dream today is gained through their service as labor migrants for the global economy. Overseas migrant workers deployed on contract and Filipinos in the Philippines with the potential of future contract work are valued for their remittances, current and future, their economic returns, enabling the maintenance of the Philippine economy and the country's role in the global order. The figure of the Filipino American immigrant operates differently. The American dream and the instrumental treatment of Filipinoness toward a greater good reconfigures under neoliberalism such that association with the privatization of social welfare and economic and individualized solutions to poverty, largely imagined as philanthropy *from* the Global North and development *in* the Global South, become markers of achievement and modern selfhood in Filipino American subjectivity. The two figures of Filipino migration and return, the Filipino American immigrant and the overseas Filipino labor migrant, both play important roles in the contemporary transnational reproduction of American exceptionalism through the terms of doing good. As participants and as subjects of national development, both figures are celebrated (or disciplined) for doing good toward the betterment of the Philippines and work in tandem to obscure the ongoing racialization of all Filipinos and the Philippine state's capture of racialized global hierarchies for global markets.

In the parlance of the Philippines, *balikbayan* and "Overseas Filipino Worker" (OFW) refer to official state and national designations of Filipino migration and citizenship for Filipino American immigrants and overseas Filipino labor migrants, respectively. *Balikbayan*, translated from Tagalog as "returnee to the nation," generally refers to Filipino American immigrants who, having left the homeland for an immigrant's life in America, return to the Philippines as visitors, tourists, or, as emphasized here, partners doing good through philanthropic projects. While not all *balikbayans* live in the United States and not all Filipinos in the United States are citizens, the dominant representation of the *balikbayan* normalizes permanent residency and U.S. citizenship status. OFW refers to migrants of laboring and professional classes who retain Philippine citizenship and work temporarily and predominantly on contract in countries all over the world. As the *balikbayan*'s discursive other, OFWs signal workers in countries other than the United States.

Literary scholar Caroline Hau, analyzing the autobiographical writing of a Filipino migrant worker in Japan and the circulation of OFW ideologies, explains that "immigration to America has long been the historical and theoretical template from which the Filipino overseas experience is hewn." As a result, dreams of overseas migration are bound to the cultural history of the "so-called American dream."[33] Also emphasizing America's position in the dreams and desires of Filipinos, Vicente Rafael notes, "Balikbayans emerge as figures to be envied. Their easy association with Western consumer products and access to a powerful state apparatus in the United States mark them as different: they represent the fulfillment of Filipino desires realizable only outside the Philippines."[34] U.S. colonial history in the Philippines created the professional systems that would funnel health professionals to the United States and nurtured the desire for U.S.-directed mobility within the Filipino population in terms of potential higher wages and participation in the American dream.[35] By keeping these systems in place, America maintains its persistent hold on the Philippine cultural imagination, a fantasy of the good life that carries implications for the Philippine state encouraging its citizens to work abroad, for the aspirations of labor migrants, and in terms of the symbolic power of the Filipino American immigrant *balikbayan.*

The two figures of Filipino migration and return embody pervasive anxieties and tensions of diaspora as well as the dreams and vulnerabilities of Filipinos. As the symbol of the abundance of what migration can offer, these associations figure the Filipino American immigrant *balikbayan* as the ultimate recompense of overseas labor migration—a transnational compensation (as in *return*) that unmoors the centrality of homeland in diasporic analysis. Identifying the ideological agenda of the state with the OFW, Hau highlights and historicizes the social relations produced in this process, suggesting that the lens of doing good allows us to theorize the materiality of diaspora:

> The overseas Filipino worker is increasingly competing with the Filipino immigrant as the discursive paradigm of overseas Filipinos experience. . . . The OFW has characteristically been viewed as a "guest worker," the terms of whose contract preclude the likelihood of permanent settlement abroad. Appearing as the "antithesis" of the Filipino-American balikbayan, the OFW is defined in terms not so much by her desire to return to the Philippines, but by the certainty of her return.[36]

Hau describes an undercurrent of Philippine nationalism, pointing to the different relationships of homeland return as a tension: the "desire to return" by the Filipino American *balikbayan* versus the "certainty" of return on the part of the OFW that guarantees the OFW's place in the national imaginary. "Return" in Hau refers to expectations of embodied return to the Philippines by Filipino migrants. However, I read the tension that Hau identifies between the Filipino American *balikbayan* and the OFW in terms of the social and cultural values placed on the differential *returns* of migration, the circulation of doing good in diaspora—of philanthropy and remittances, respectively, for the two figures. These forms of doing good correspond to moral valuations of giving that endow Filipino American immigrants with partnership in national economic development, but overseas Filipino labor migrants with obligatory economic duty. Returns encapsulate the moral and emotional investments of individuals, diasporas, and the nation. Unlike Filipino American *balikbayans*, however, overseas Filipino labor migrants are cast as people who cannot be left to themselves to choose to do good; their returns must be ensured rather than chosen, warranting guidance and monitoring from the state and the national culture.

Desirous of but not required to return, Filipino American immigrants are at liberty to choose to return or not, positioning all of their returns as an economic bonus for the Philippines. If the Filipino American *balikbayan*'s return to the Philippines is motivated by the personal desire to return, returns are not obligated or structured by the neoliberal global economy. This casts all Filipino American giving practices in a philanthropic light. The Filipino American immigrant *balikbayan* as bearer of the American dream maintains maneuverability in entering the Philippine national imaginary because it is an expatriate's choice to remain loyal. As an individual who has achieved the good life in America, the Filipino American immigrant has the liberty to choose what to do with that success. Even remittances sent from Filipino Americans are seen as freely given gifts. One columnist for a major Philippine newspaper emphasizes this in his representation of Filipino Americans as exemplary diasporans:

> There is a cliché which says the worth of a person is not what he owns, but what he gives. Records show that Filipino-Americans remitted $8 billion to the Philippines in 2009, representing almost 60% of all remittances by Overseas Filipinos (OFs) and Overseas Filipino Workers (OFWs). . . . It is time that we confront what weakens us and find deliberate ways to dismantle them by setting a course to *let the best in us lead the way*. . . . The sterling example of Filipino-Americans in lending a consistent helping hand symbolized by an $8 billion remittance to relatives in the motherland is an affirmation that they continue to love the Philippines.[37]

Here, Filipino American remittances are cloaked in the discourse of desiring to do good. The imagery of "lending a consistent helping hand" makes Filipino American remittances all the more precious because they are voluntary. Because Filipino Americans set the "sterling example" for all Filipinos, the negative aspects of Filipino culture alluded to by the author correlate to the OFW. Larger calls for all Filipinos to support the nation mask how differences are produced in the meanings placed on migration and returns and how mobility and social privilege transpire in the interplay between the institutionalization of state categories of migration and the terms of diasporic return.

Memorializing Returns from Abroad

Through presidential order, agencies of the Philippines maintain two separate awards programs for overseas Filipino labor migrants and Filipino American immigrants who give back to the country and participate in national development. These awards acknowledge the sacrifice and commitment to the homeland that national discourse expects of its emigrants and migrants, allowing them to stand in for the nation. Together they demonstrate the operations of the purportedly collective commitment to the official history of diaspora, migration, and returns. The awards programs define history in terms of sacrifice and gratitude of both overseas Filipino labor migrants and Filipino American immigrants, obscuring demands of obligation, the interests of the national economy, Filipinos' various responses to these demands, and the power of the American dream. The awards memorialize the stakes of giving back to the homeland, best understood as the transnational negotiations of doing good, and conceal logics of neoliberal globalization in the reproduction of diaspora.

The Philippine Overseas Employment Administration (POEA), one of the government agencies that processes contracts of Filipinos who work abroad, maintains a state-sanctioned awards program for Filipino migrants, Bagong Bayani Awards or the New Heroes Awards: "The awards seek to recognize and pay tribute to our OFWs for their significant efforts in fostering goodwill among peoples of the world, enhancing and promoting the image of the Filipino as a competent, responsible and dignified worker."[38] The OFW named here is an ambassador for the Philippines who embodies the affective possibilities of doing good. The POEA presents awards in different categories, including the Bagong Bayani Award for Outstanding Employee, whose criteria include "manifested love for work, concern for the company and his or her co-workers," displaying for the international community the diligence of its labor exports and rewarding its migrant citizens for internalizing the dictates of neoliberal and capitalist orthodoxy that promote their role as compliant labor.[39] Recipients of the Bagong Bayani Award for Community and Social Service include those who "have performed heroic act or deed, or have saved life or property, the performance of which is beyond the normal call of duty."[40] Larger discussions of community or social service, for which the award is named, are subsumed in the celebration of individual acts of heroism abstracted from the material relations of their labor and migration. The 2011 Bagong Bayani Awards provide a startling example of the implications of heroism, the dominant discourse of Filipino labor migration that requires individual sacrifice for the nation. Naming that year's recipients, former president Benigno Aquino III describes the actions and values that garnered the attention for these overseas Filipino labor migrants: "During the height of the tragedy in Fukushima, several brave, compassionate Filipino caregivers and nurses refused to abandon their patients at the height of the crisis."[41] "Despite imminent danger and risk of nuclear radiation," one newspaper article notes, overseas Filipino labor migrants "chose to remain in their jobs and continue to provide care and companionship to their elderly Japanese patients."[42] The awards commend bodily sacrifice, naturalizing it as part of migrant Filipino life. Naming labor migrants the new heroes of the country silences the disruptions, insecurities, and violence of overseas labor migration.

The 2011 Bagong Bayani Awards extend the ironies of doing good. This particular celebration of the overseas Filipino labor migrant flips the dominant script of rescue. Instead of recognizing another poor Filipino to be rescued by the good deeds of others, the Philippine government commemorates overseas Filipino labor migrants who are willing to rescue their employers regardless of the dangers posed to their own lives and to the networks of people who depend on their continued labor and remittances. The object of rescue is not a fellow countryman, as one might expect in a formal acknowledgment of the Philippines' labor diaspora, but the employer, the symbolism of which reassures future employers that the Philippines, the labor-sending state, mandates that the sacrifices performed by overseas Filipino labor migrants are not just for the benefit of one's family or even the homeland but also for the global economy and the Philippines' place in that order.

Filipino American immigrants, as I illustrate, are differently structured and hence differently celebrated for their practices of doing good. The Commission on Filipinos Overseas (CFO) of the Office of the President maintains links with Filipino permanent residents and citizens of foreign countries. Originally created to surveil anti-Marcos activists and exiles in the United States, the CFO's primary purpose today is to facilitate philanthropy, medical aid, and social-development assistance from overseas Filipinos. Donations and humanitarian efforts are made almost entirely by Filipino Americans. In its literature, the organization asks, "What role does the CFO play in encouraging overseas Filipinos to promote national development?" To this, the CFO responds:

> Pursuant to its mandate, CFO develops and implements activities that facilitate the flow of assistance from Filipinos overseas to local communities in the Philippines. Through the CFO's *Lingkod sa Kapwa Pilipino* (LINKAPIL) or Link for Philippine Development Program, overseas Filipinos are able to support livelihood/micro-enterprise development, education, health and welfare, small-scale infrastructure, and technology and skills transfer. CFO also maintains active linkages with Filipino associations and other potential donors overseas, as well as local partners in the Philippines, to encourage investments and partnerships for development.[43]

In 1991 President Corazon Aquino, Ferdinand Marcos's successor, instituted a government policy to celebrate overseas Filipinos and organizations, mostly from the United States, that support philanthropic, humanitarian, or social-development projects in the Philippines. This policy calls for the CFO and the Department of Foreign

Affairs to award plaques and medallions to select "Filipino individuals and organizations overseas who have contributed materially—or in the form of selfless programs and endeavors—to our country's relief, rehabilitation, and development programs," with the knowledge that "it is socially desirable and in the national interest to provide a permanent system of recognition for the valuable contributions being made to our developmental concerns by our countrymen and organizations abroad."[44] Four categories of Presidential Awards are bestowed for exceptional contribution to the reconstruction, progress, and development in the Philippines and to Filipinos who "have brought the country honor."[45] From 1991 to 2010, the CFO conferred thirty-seven Link for Philippine Development Awards, thirty of which went to Filipino Americans or Filipino American organizations. This government agency monitors and awards overseas Filipinos, most of whom live in the United States, who take their own initiative to identify or develop projects in the Philippines that assist the poor and needy. It constructs the Filipino American immigrant as a transnational safety net for the local population whose needs the government is unable to meet despite its programs for labor migration.

In its current economic structuring, the Philippine state needs the outflow of overseas Filipino labor migrants. In a 2013 World Bank study, of the 500,000 college graduates in the Philippines that entered the labor force every year during the previous decade, "only 240,000 found jobs in the country's formal sector and . . . 200,000 found work abroad."[46] As Antoinette Raquiza notes, "Based on such analysis, one can draw out the importance that overseas employment has come to play in expanding the consumer market."[47] At the same time, it is the figure of the Filipino American immigrant that drives the dream of living abroad. The nation-state normalizes and institutionalizes both the *balikbayan* and the OFW, containing radicalism and revolutionary elements of the population by propping up the Philippines' role in neoliberal globalization as the world's supplier of cheap labor. Because of differences in citizenship, the Philippine state must differently guide Filipino American immigrant and overseas Filipino labor migrant giving practices, yet it guides them toward the shared goal of national economic development, producing distinct state subjects yet united toward official national development goals. The language of community service, selfless endeavors, sacrifice, and development "reinforces the state as a moral institution, providing guidance on how to behave" in migration and returns.[48]

Genealogies and the Cultural Politics of Doing Good

In 1973, less than a year into martial law and the experiment with a New Society, Ferdinand Marcos instigated "Operation Homecoming," actively courting Filipino expatriates abroad to visit the Philippines, promising reduced airfares, subsidized vacation packages, and expedited entry processes and officially inaugurating the term *balikbayan*, or "returnee." Marcos created his *balikbayan* program to address the political and economic concerns over the implementation of martial law and accusations of repression and corruption. At that time, the vast majority of Filipinos living outside the Philippines resided in the United States. The oil boom in the Middle East that lasted until the mid-1980s and depended on temporary migrant labor was just beginning, and the global phenomenon of overseas Filipino labor migrants, particularly the "feminization" of this labor formation, had yet to emerge. Marcos encouraged the Filipino American immigrant *balikbayan* to return and visit the Philippines as a tourist whose money spent on vacation would be an investment in the tourism economy that he was desperate to build. Through implicit support by Filipino Americans, Marcos also hoped to assuage international concern regarding his usurpation of power. As stated by Marcos's minister of tourism, "Every visit is an endorsement of the continuation of the political, economic, and social stability achieved by . . . martial law."[49] With the *balikbayan*, Marcos attempted to transform Filipinos in the United States into an overseas community, discursively united through a common orientation toward the Philippines, identified with a common institutional category, and serving a particular purpose for the martial-law state. The *balikbayan* as tourist and social-development agent began with Operation Homecoming, but the discourse persists today. Many Filipino Americans understand their homeland tourist returns as a form of doing good from diaspora. For example, in response to a general question I posed about how Filipinos in the United States could best help Filipinos in the Philippines, one Filipino American association and community leader responded that Filipinos need to have pride in coming from the Philippines and that this pride should lead to vacations "back home": "We can have this pride in being from the Philippines and helping them [in the Philippines] at the same time. Economically, we take vacations there, and we spend money there and spend dollars there."[50]

The desire to return is paralleled by the desire for consumerist returns to the Philippines from the United States:

> There's nothing like receiving a big cardboard box full of goodies or pasalubong [gifts brought back to the Philippines from travel to other destinations] from relatives overseas. It's the warm feeling Manny Paez remembers when he was younger growing up in the Philippines. "I used to tear open the cardboard box and hang them up along my walls so my friends could see that I'm receiving gifts from my family in the U.S.," said Paez. That was decades ago for Paez but the feeling remains the same for many people in the Philippines. . . . While most [migrants] send money back home to their family, it's the balikbayan box that adds an extra touch like adding whipped cream on an ice cream sundae.[51]

Though the *balikbayan* box is a welcome arrival, the pressure to bring gifts to family and friends in the Philippines may prevent the Filipino American from returning to the Philippines at all. Emphasizing the potential costs of such returns, one respondent, Georgie Cruz, declares:

> It's always a problem when you give. You give to feel good. You give to help. You give to have control. When you give to your hometown, think about what are you announcing. To tell people that you are better off than when you left. Like the *pasalubong* [the gifts brought to the Philippines]. I would talk to other Filipinos [in the United States]: "Why don't you go back to the Philippines to visit?" And they always said, "Oh, it's too expensive." "But you take vacations to Florida." And they said, "It's the *pasalubong* that is so expensive."[52]

Filipino American immigrant returns are always understood in relation to the returns of overseas Filipino labor migrants. Overseas

Filipino labor migrants are the "real heroes," explains a Filipino American physical therapist. "They remit almost all their earnings, while we (immigrants) only send some money to show relatives we are still important."[53] Filipino American immigrant returns deviate significantly from the sacrifice of migration for overseas Filipino labor migrants, the heroes of the nation in their willingness to work abroad, to remit a large portion of earnings, and to even put their lives at risk so that returns can be made. For Filipino American immigrants, returns to the homeland are premised on expectations of the distribution of gifts and consumer items in the Philippines, the objects for which they are envied. The transmutation from philanthropic or charitable gifts to consumer-based gifts, described by Georgie Cruz, distinguishes Filipino American immigrant difference naturalized through doing good. Notions of giving informed by individualism and consumer-based giving discourage Filipino American immigrants from considering what they share with overseas Filipino labor migrants and with impoverished Filipinos in the Philippines, while simultaneously elevating the Filipino American immigrant as bearer of the American dream.

Support for philanthropic projects by Filipino American immigrants to the Philippines is an integral aspect of their identities, reflecting the value-laden nature of diaspora. The following description of giving from one Filipino American hometown association implies that potential future giving drives the desire to migrate out of the Philippines and to the United States in the first place:

> The activities of the Angeleños in Southern California [are] simply not limited to religious and social function. To the Angeleños migrating to [a] foreign land is not the end in itself but serves as a means to pursue the common goodness of providing [a] better future for their families. And in return share their blessings to the needy. The association provide[s] educational assistance to deserving children of Angeleños back home impaired by financial difficulties.[54]

Beneficent returns and doing good in diaspora justify the idealized position of the Filipino American immigrant, making migration meaningful to one's family and to the homeland. Financial pressures to migrate, imperialist fantasies of America, and the global economy's racialization of Filipinos are supplanted by the purported desire to philanthropically give. Differences in migration and socioeconomic mobility come to reflect one's own proclivities toward doing good as a Filipino diasporan, proclivities that are learned in America but created and naturalized in the transformation from Filipino to Filipino migrant to Filipino American immigrant *balikbayan*. An active Filipino American organization president stated:

> I wasn't raised with exposure to volunteerism. *Bayanihan* [mutual assistance or community spirit] is just a gimmick for us. There is just a trace of that. I only saw it once, moving the house of a squatter. At the end of the project, there was rice soup with banana and *kamote* [a type of sweet potato]. There is no such thing as volunteerism in the Philippines. We don't have that in our schools. Here in the United States, you can get extra credit [in school] if you volunteer more. [*He then showed me a newspaper clipping of children being trained to help volunteer with tsunami relief.*] When there was flooding [in the Philippines], no one helped each other. Either relatives helped them or no one did. The culture is that we don't know who to follow. If you are rich, then you think that is your place, so you don't help others. It's the crab mentality. If I'm not rich, I don't expect help. If [a] family is rich, they wouldn't invite the poor relations.[55]

The value of giving outside one's family characterizes the transformation from Filipino to Filipino American immigrant, demonstrating how this figure is differentiated from others those Filipinos who require their assistance.

While the Filipino American immigrant is encouraged to do good out of values related to volunteerism and a good society, the Philippine state maintains greater power to fix the terms of doing good for the overseas Filipino labor migrant who remains a citizen of the country. For over four decades and following the changing dynamics of global capital, migration, and development, the Philippine state has sought to control the ways that labor migrants, as designated by visas and contracts, give back, affecting how migrants are structured as agents in relationship to national development. The Marcos government in 1982 institutionalized the overseas Filipino labor migrant's "certainty" of returns when it required migrant workers to remit 50 to 80 percent of their earnings through authorized channels, controlling the exchange rates and holding passport renewals until migrant workers submitted proof of remittance returns.[56] Migrant workers protested these conditions of labor and giving, and the government devised a scheme to mask state power. Former president Corazon Aquino's government shifted direct control of remittances onto the terrain of national culture. Instead of a state mandate, a discourse of heroism was developed to celebrate overseas Filipino labor migrants for their sacrifice and departure. In more recent descriptions of nationalism's power over remittances, members of the Philippine government attempt to downplay its reliance on its citizens' participation in overseas labor migration by emphasizing that overseas Filipino labor migrants have choices regarding migration and remittance returns. The government's emphasis on choice attempts to define overseas migration and remittances through the individual agency of each current and potential migrant, minimizing how much the government depends on remittances for economic survival and labor export as a strategy for the containment of popular unrest. The state facilitates overseas labor migration, and it must simultaneously attempt to control the political, economic, and social linkages that overseas Filipino migrants maintain with the Philippines to perpetuate their participation in the global economy. This diasporic relationship is primarily premised on giving remittances to one's immediate family and supported by the country's commitment to supplying the "Great Filipino Worker," an expression attributed to former president Gloria Macapagal Arroyo, to almost every country in the world.[57]

Where Filipino American immigrant consumer practices are to be envied, discourses related to overseas Filipino labor migrant consumer practices often conjure deviant subjects, an ideological construction that exists alongside their depiction as heroes. Official and popular discourses construct overseas labor migrants as heroes for their willingness to work abroad. Their sacrifice is in removing themselves from their homes and their families so that they can participate in remittance returns. However, government officials and policy analysts criticize overseas Filipino labor migrants for their conspicuous consumption. When they or their families to whom their earnings are remitted purchase consumer goods, it is described as being at the expense of investments that may be more beneficial to economic development and the financialization of capital. As a people who have yet to achieve the good life, overseas Filipino labor migrants are not permitted by national discourse to appear as if they are doing *too* well. For example, sociologist Shu-Ju Ada Cheng writes, "Scholars and government officials have questioned whether the remittance [from overseas Filipino labor migrants] has been effective in facilitating national development, since the money sent home has often been used for 'conspicuous consumption,' such as buying land, setting up small businesses, or purchasing consumer goods, rather than for investments conducive to economic growth."[58] In their displays of consumer-based returns to the homeland, Filipino American immigrants demonstrate the material achievements of the American dream. However, accusations of conspicuous consumption are lodged against overseas Filipino labor migrants and not Filipino American immigrants because of state claims to their economic returns. Given that overseas Filipino labor migrants are produced in tense relationship to the figure of the Filipino American immigrant and given the discourse of conspicuous consumers that, along with remittances, mark the terms of their doing good, it is understood to be the Filipino American immigrant, or restrained consumer, to whom the overseas Filipino labor migrant is placed in comparison.

Conclusion

The number of overseas Filipinos and their remittances demonstrates that Filipino Americans, while simultaneously counted and then elided in larger conversations on Filipino labor migration, figure prominently in the anxieties that surround nationalism, migration, and giving practices, alternately represented as remittances, philanthropy, or support of economic development. In masking the disastrous impact of the Philippines' neoliberal policies, the production of the docile Filipino migrant laborer as readily available for the international market contains the threat of radical social transformation. Robyn Rodriguez highlights this direct link in the history of the state's shift to labor broker: "Marcos violently suppressed the growing communist movement, which was at the forefront of the struggle to depose his dictatorship. He saw the export of labor as an important measure to curb the political unrest likely to be exacerbated by un- and underemployment."[59] Overseas employment mutes radical political aspirations and organizing energies. Walden Bello, a prolific scholar on the Global South, and his colleagues state that overseas workers "might otherwise have gone into [a] radical or revolutionary solution and, in economic terms, an external employment mechanism in the absence of development."[60] Overseas labor migration disciplines its subjects toward the economic interests of the state and in opposition to movements that would require a sustained analysis of the political-economic structure of the Philippines. Deviant citizens are reformed as overseas Filipino labor migrants who are ushered out of the country, while the Filipino American immigrant, similarly contained and depoliticized, is anointed for efforts to uplift those less fortunate.

Ironically, former secretary of labor and employment Patricia Santo Tomas reverses the state's disciplining of its migrant citizens, stating that Filipinos would revolt if overseas labor migration was taken away: "I've always viewed [overseas employment] as a safety valve. . . . If you prevent them from going to Hong Kong or Saudi Arabia, you might have a revolution on your hands."[61] Overseas labor migration, when constructed as a right, becomes rewritten as the will of the people. As a potential trigger for revolution, it is something that *they* are willing to fight for; it is something that *they* see as their fundamental right as humans or as Filipinos. However, as a stabilizing mechanism for social unrest, labor migration ultimately benefits the state and its economic interests and allies. In Santo Tomas's reversal, Filipino labor migrants are doubly contained. Their potential for radical revolutionary movements is restricted by the promise of overseas migration, and their earnings are leveraged in the service of national development policies, thus emphasizing not the economic dimensions of remittances but rather the political-cultural implications, where the overseas migrant worker is commodified by the state.

The goal of radical containment similarly affects the Filipino American immigrant. This can be seen in a conversation with a manager of the CFO, who describes this agency as originally initiated by the Marcos government to monitor political exiles in the United

States.[62] After the termination of the Marcos regime, the CFO transformed its objectives so that instead of monitoring exiles and their radical and/or communist politics, it now courts Filipino American donations to national economic development projects as *partners* with the state as development agents.

The discursive archetypes of Filipino migration and returns circulate in popular discourse as separate categories of diasporic experience. However, the symbolic construction of the Filipino American immigrant *balikbayan* enables the Philippines' success as a labor-brokering state. The possibility of permanent residency in the United States is used as a carrot that drives Filipinos toward overseas labor migration and the Philippines' contributions to the global economy. The American dream operates transnationally and structures trajectories of labor migration characterized by an elusive transformation from Filipino to Filipino American immigrant, producing competing diasporas between those who have made it in America, Filipino American immigrants, against those who hope to make it one day, overseas Filipino labor migrants, who may, in practice, agree to work in a stepping-stone country while ostensibly maintaining the hope of achieving *balikbayan* status. While the overseas Filipino labor migrant may appear as the antithesis of the Filipino American *balikbayan*, these figures are mutually constituted, "drawing their discursive legibility and social power in relation to one another."[63] From the onset, doing good tethers both figures and their legibility in the national landscape. The Philippine state produced and institutionalized these categories of migration and returns in ways that served the needs of their respective historical and political economic moments, with lasting effects on how migration and homeland returns are imagined today.

2

Homeland Disorientations

Toward Antidevelopmentalist Diaspora-Giving Politics

Chapter 1 suggests that constructed divisions within the Filipino diaspora, particularly between the figures of the Filipino American *balikbayan* and the OFW, serve as a force for global capital and alibi for the exclusions inherent in the American dream. Diaspora-giving discourse—both popular and official state—can distract us from identifying and engaging transnational labor issues, thus narrowing the possibilities of diaspora politics in problematic ways. Moving away from the cultural work of diasporic returns, this chapter focuses on the multiplicity of homes and homeland orientations as dimensions of diasporic life.

U.S.-based Filipina novelist, journalist, activist, and organizer Ninotchka Rosca, in interviews both printed and with me, proposes a diasporic framework of social transformation that accounts for the consequences of the Philippine economy's dependence on labor migration.[1] Rosca critically examines the meaning of home that is produced in the institutionalization of labor migration. She connects the Philippines' policies of out-migration to the bifurcation of migrant Filipino subjectivities, a temporal, spatial, and psychic split created by a personal and collective sense of transience. The Philippine program for economic development institutionalizes circular migration, which occurs when Filipinos, whose mobility is controlled by the terms set by guest-worker programs, overseas work contracts, and temporary-stay visas, move to work outside the country, return to the Philippines when the terms of the job expire, and then repeat. Rosca argues that the celebration of the economic and cosmopolitan opportunities created by globalization is a convenient framing of circular migration for imperialism: "The notion that circular migration is positive because it creates 'transnational' people is convenient for imperialism as it hides the trap of impermanence for migrant workers who are forced to move from country back to home and out again. . . . The condition of impermanence created by circular migration justifies disengagement from the politics of the receiving country and from the need and duty to create change wherever we find ourselves."[2] Thus, Filipino migrants do not develop place-based politics, preventing all but the most activist-minded migrants to risk their livelihoods and their security by engaging local issues. The subjectification of Filipino migrants leads to a singular orientation to home, to a wholeness that can be achieved only back home and apart from where one lives and works. This bifurcation contributes to a state of deferment of political agency for migrant subjects to some future time and place when work, family, and home align. Moreover, it contributes to the power of exclusionary nativist nationalisms that benefit from the singular orientation of migrants, conditioned by impermanence, to their own homelands and not to the homes and nations where they temporarily reside.

Rosca argues that this singular orientation toward the homeland is a convenience for imperialism. Oriented toward the homeland in their daily lives, nativist nationalisms instruct migrant subjects to see their struggles as migrants from the Philippines as disconnected from their struggles as workers in the countries in which they live. Conditioned by impermanence, Filipino migrant subjects are removed from those categories of people who are allowed to apprehend the world as agents of change.[3]

Both Filipino migrant workers and Filipino immigrants live under this condition of bifurcation. While Filipino American U.S. citizens and permanent residents are protected from the trap of impermanence, as identified by Rosca, disengagement from the politics of the receiving country bolsters the global order in tandem with the Philippine export of laborers. Filipino Americans exist in bifurcation when they understand their political lives, or how they understand the context and direction of their political agency, as separate from their lives and presence in the United States. To be clear, however, bifurcated Filipino American subjectivities are not simply a result of working and living in the United States and then directing commitments to social transformation primarily to the Philippines. Rather, dominant diasporic homeland orientations from Filipino America and to the Philippine homeland bifurcate immigrant subjectivities when based on the unidirectionality of social transformation, when philanthropy and social development are imagined in diaspora as endeavors to be implemented in the homeland, as concerning social or environmental problems located in a bounded space back home. Official bilateral and multilateral development programs have a clear unidirectionality, where aid originates in the Global North and flows to the Global South, with conditions stipulated by the Global North and motivated by extractive global capitalist logics. Filipino Americans consent to their bifurcation when oriented toward a Philippine homeland through the belief that these projects of social transformation are outside the messiness and divisiveness of politics and transnational injustice. While allowed to be bearers of knowledge of the political and economic machinations back home, the cost is the denial of, in Rosca's words, "the need and duty to create change wherever we find ourselves" within contexts of diasporic politics. This denial of the immigrants' responsibility to understand social transformation through the places where they find themselves maintains a space for developmentalist logics to thrive in diaspora giving. Acknowledging the hegemony of developmentalist logics in diasporic practice, the aim of this chapter is to theorize a politics of diasporic *homeland disorientation* to disrupt developmentalism in diaspora and to offer a *homeland reorientation* toward counterhegemonic forms of diaspora giving. Developmentalism is an orientation toward a global reality in which the ultimate objective is, ostensibly, a global state of development. As an orientation, it catalogues social relationships and locations, referring to both a mode of existence and the unidirectionality of social, political, and economic commitments and concern. For developmentalism, the mode of existence is one that erases the historical emergence of development.

Official development, which is an ordering of the world, operates under the assumption that it exists outside politics. Arif Dirlik writes that developmentalism, carefully distinguished from development, refers to "an ideological *orientation* characterized by the fetishization of development, or the attribution to development of the power of a natural (or even divine) force which humans can resist or question only at the risk of being condemned to stagnation and poverty. The ideology renders opaque the historical forces that have shaped the idea of development. It also disguises the social and political forces that have played, and continue to play, a crucial part in endowing it with the power to dominate human consciousness."[4] I find Dirlik's approach to developmentalism generative to a specifically diasporic analysis because it helps in characterizing a contemporary and conservative Filipino American homeland orientation. It suggests the need to outline the discursive, historical, political, and social consequences of this orientation as an imperative of diasporic practice. Development and diaspora both involve ideological orientations, and developmentalism and dominant diaspora-giving practices both fetishize development.

The diasporic fetishization of development occurs when social-development and philanthropic projects correlate to an apolitical or antipolitical orientation toward the Philippines. The social and political forces that lead to the celebration of philanthropy and social development for its own sake, thereby universalizing the goodness of these abstract practices, create a collective distrust of practices that exceed developmentalist logics. In particular, practices and participation in movements deemed too activist or too political for their sustained critique of U.S. imperialism and global capitalism are brushed aside during serious conversations about Philippine futures in a dominant homeland orientation.

Social development and philanthropy guide the collective homeland orientation of the Filipino American diaspora, but this has not always been the measure of diasporic belonging. A communal conviction to better or improve the lives of those in the Philippines through social development and philanthropy follows a previous moment of Filipino American diasporic history wherein Filipino American organizations and activists assembled in protest of martial law in the Philippines, which was declared by Ferdinand Marcos in 1972. While many would like to consider the Marcos era a historical relic, Marcos's widow, Imelda, their children, and their partners in government pilfering gained and maintained powerful political positions through the decades and continue to receive enormous support from the current president, Rodrigo Duterte. There has been no end to the era of Marcos.

I take two lessons from the Filipino American anti–martial law movement for this examination of diaspora giving. First, the bifurcation of Filipino America led to the dissolution of almost every Filipino American organization working in solidarity with the Philippine Left in the years following Marcos's exile. Diaspora-giving critique can learn from these collective failures. Second, the anti–martial law movement that emerged in response to Marcos's abuse of power determined the collective homeland orientation of Filipino America of its time. The fall of Marcos presaged an apolitical and sometimes antipolitical Filipino American homeland orientation. Social development was celebrated as a remedy to the laboriousness and divisiveness of years of antimartial organizing.

Ninotchka Rosca's forty-five-year political work spans national borders and conscientiously responds to regime change in the Philippines, the global rise of neoliberalism, and the state's shifting demands of its migrant population. I turn to Rosca's ideas to elaborate on the relationship between martial law and Filipino American diasporic history and homeland orientations and how that relationship can counter the force of development. Her international anti-imperialist politics and organizing began in college, where she protested the Vietnam War and Ferdinand Marcos's pledge to the United States to send combat engineers to support the U.S. military in Vietnam. After Marcos declared martial law, Rosca was imprisoned and violently interrogated five times. Once released, Rosca took a writer's fellowship at the University of Iowa, never ceasing in her anti–martial law and pro-revolutionist organizing. Preparing to return to the Philippines at the conclusion of her fellowship, Rosca heard that she was on the Marcos regime's arrest list once again. Fearing for her life, Rosca filed for political asylum in the United States, where she continues to live, write, work, and organize. The evolution of her politics offers a way of imagining counterhegemonic giving practices and commitments that respond to historically specific contexts without capitulating to the needs of U.S. imperialism or of global capital.

To explore homeland orientation, and the temporality and directionality of diaspora giving, this chapter turns its attention to martial law in the Philippines and Filipino American homeland orientation since the 1970s. The chapter explores the consequences of a singular homeland orientation and identifies the transformation of collective Filipino American orientation from a period of anti–martial law to a period of philanthropy and development. I analyze Rosca's political discourse as an alternative homeland orientation to one structured by developmentalist logics and the bifurcation of Filipino American lives. Through her decades of political work, Rosca has fostered a transnational, feminist politics useful in identifying dominant assumptions of home as well as nondevelopmentalist temporalities. I read Rosca's political writing and my interviews with her as highlighting an important example of diaspora-giving practice that works against the imperialist divisions of global and diasporic space.

Martial Law and Filipino American Diasporic Homeland Orientation

After Ferdinand Marcos declared martial law in the Philippines on September 23, 1972, his enforcers immediately began detaining those who posed or were suspected of posing a threat to the government. Politicians, judges, lawyers, student activists, and journalists were imprisoned, along with suspected members of the recently formed Communist Party of the Philippines (CPP) and the insurgent New People's Army. Marcos used the threat of communist control and disruption as his justification for martial law and promised the nation that the powers gained by suspending the constitution would provide the latitude to "liquidate [the] Communist apparatus."[5] In the following months and years, the human rights abuses committed by Marcos's government intensified and continued without censure from the U.S. government. Economic instability in the Philippines also intensified, which grew alongside the wealth of the Marcos clan and its supporters. U.S. political support began to fade before the end of the Marcos dictatorship because of economic volatility, concerns about the nation's enormous national debt, and the regime's failure to provide a secure environment for the continuance of the American military installments at Clark Air Force Base and Subic Naval Base.[6] Ferdinand Marcos was ousted in 1986, fleeing with his family to eventually arrive in Hawai'i for his life (and death) in exile.

From within Filipino America, anti–martial law leaders, organizers, and activists, including those who secured official asylum in the United States, responded with indictments that matched the range of social ills attributed to the Marcos dictatorship. Much of the academic writing on the anti–martial law movement focuses on one particular U.S.-based organization working in affiliation with the CPP, the Katipunan ng nga Demokratikong Pilipino (Union of Democratic Filipinos [KDP]), which Helen Toribio describes as "the most organized leftist institution in the history of the Filipino American community."[7] The KDP was created after founding members abandoned the National Coalition for the Restoration of Civil Liberties in the Philippines (NCRCLP), which established what some describe as politically moderate aims. The NCRCLP brought together a broad-based coalition of Filipino American organizations that constituted the anti–martial law movement and "united around the principles of 1) opposition to martial law, 2) restoration of civil liberties, 3) release of political prisoners, and 4) end of U.S. support to Marcos."[8] The NCRCLP, however, could not contain conflicting ideological and political commitments of member groups. Cold war anticommunism clashed with radicalism. Commitments to restore pre–martial law status quo clashed with revolutionary and national democratic politics. Filipino American groups splintered over hearsay and misunderstanding, and personal relationships dissolved as individuals battled over the priorities and mission of the anti–martial law movement.

An uneasy relationship developed between the CPP and the KDP because of the racial and class inequalities experienced by Filipino American activists, who understood their experiences as both Filipinos and racial minorities in the United States, and the CPP's demands regarding commitments for national democracy in the Philippines. In response, the U.S.-based KDP delineated what it characterized as the "dual line" program, combining revolutionary politics, an anti–martial law agenda, and attention to American racism and discriminatory policies. In the words of Marco Cuevas-Hewitt, "No longer did diasporans only see themselves as overseas Filipinos but, increasingly, also as racialised minorities within the U.S. The question of race was incorporated into KDP's class analysis becoming one of the core issues of its socialist programme."[9]

The CPP attempted to transform the KDP into an overseas chapter of its own organization; it demanded that the KDP prioritize "the revolutionary struggle of the Filipino people against the U.S.-Marcos dictatorship" above all else.[10] In doing so, the CPP reduced, according to intellectual historian Augusto Espiritu, "U.S. Filipinos to Philippine nationals rather than as a diverse group that might have social identities distinct from those of Philippine nationals. In hindsight, one is astounded by the lack of analysis of the long histories of U.S. colonialism and racism and especially their impact on Filipino migrants."[11] There was no recognition or support from the Philippine-based CPP for Filipino American struggles over affirmative action, discrimination against foreign-trained professionals, union reform, or housing issues. These were pressing U.S.-based Filipino American struggles, but they created tensions with organizers in the Philippines. Both organizations failed to respond in a way that could relieve the problematic bifurcated existence that Rosca bemoans.

The anti–martial law movement marked a significant moment in Filipino American diasporic history. It strove to unite disconnected communities through a common homeland goal and through a process that brought together multiple levels and intensities of politics through a denunciation of Marcos's regime. Philanthropy and social development, I argue, have replaced the anti–martial law politics of the early to mid-1980s in an overdetermination of diasporic orientations and transnational politics. "Goodwill" has become the primary goal of homeland orientation and diaspora politics since the end of the martial-law movement, thus conveying the notion that the only social, political, or cultural values involved in philanthropy and development are good intentions.

On the fortieth anniversary of the declaration of martial law in 2012, the *Philippine Daily Inquirer* published a piece on Filipino Americans who came together to fight the martial-law regime in the Philippines. In this article, anti–martial law activist Edwin Batongbacal explains, "Martial Law was significant because it was the first organized time the community united around a higher aspiration for the country."[12] Some may argue that this was not the birth of Filipino American diasporic history or the first time that Filipinos in the United States united in their orientation toward the homeland. For example, one could argue that Filipino migrant laborers in the 1930s on the West Coast of the United States had a collective homeland orientation and organizing structure to call for independence of the Philippines from the United States. My interest here is in how the post-Marcos era channels this "higher aspiration for the country" described by Batongbacal.

Dominant Filipino American homeland orientation rests mostly on the notion that the political side of anti–martial law organizing can be, should be, and *is* abandoned in Filipino American–initiated philanthropy and social-development projects in the Philippines. The diaspora thus becomes a desired haven for the apolitical. The anti–martial law movement had significant ideological divisions, and it was spurred by the violence and repression of the Marcos regime and the awareness that the U.S. government had played a significant part in legitimizing martial law. Today, the target of organizing has become more amorphous, and a discourse of goodwill has become the dominant feature of diasporic belonging. Instead of a single identifiable antagonist, previously embodied by Ferdinand Marcos, Filipino Americans now turn toward conceptual phenomena with no clear origins or singular figure to blame: poverty, corruption, hunger, or underdevelopment in the Philippines. I take issue with neither the specific social development and philanthropic projects that Filipino Americans implement in the Philippines nor the intentions of individual Filipino Americans who donate their time and money to those projects. My concern focuses on the consequences of dominant homeland orientations in diaspora giving.

Marcos's tenure in Malacañang played out during a time of radical shifts in the global political economy. A shift in postwar development during the 1970s led to free-market policy and the World Bank–led export-oriented policies that restructured the third world. The idea of official development was born in the post–World War II "project of intervention in the 'third world' that emerged in the context of decolonization and the cold war," which Gillian Hart usefully differentiates from nonofficial or "small d" development, referring to "the development of capitalism as a geographically uneven, profoundly contradictory set of historical processes."[13] Marcos gladly played his role in institutionalizing official development, accepting IMF loans, in part, to cover debt repayments from his extravagant spending. Structural adjustment policy and conditional lending eventually met enormous criticism from the international community, particularly for its lack of analysis and efforts to target those who suffered most acutely from widespread poverty. The austerity measures of official development had propelled and integrated the neoliberal ideology of economic and political systems since the late 1970s, and by softening official development by the late 1980s to explicitly address poverty as well as gender equity and human rights, development experts of the multilateral agencies helped reframe these ongoing issues as the responsibility of development policy.[14] Poverty, gender inequity, and labor exploitation were not seen as intrinsic to the ruling economic and political systems but rather as problems that could be solved through development expertise and programs, led by the development agencies that sprang from these same ruling economic and political systems. Relatedly, a trend toward the neoliberal privatization of social welfare and the current role of international NGOs as the primary mechanism for "delivering development and addressing poverty in place of the state" took hold in the 1980s, which saw the intensification of "market-led approaches to development, and individual and agency approaches to poverty alleviation."[15] Filipino America integrated this framework of transformation, which resulted in a post-Marcos developmentalist diasporic homeland orientation.

The Antipolitics of Diaspora Giving

Two months after Ferdinand Marcos's exile from the Philippines in 1986, the *New York Times* published an article with testimonials by professional Filipinos in the United States—immigrants and exiles from the Philippine political elite who were forced to leave the country during martial law. Imagining a stark post-Marcos moment through rupture or break from politics, the article deploys a diasporic discourse that enables the normalization of developmentalism. Its celebration of an antipolitical, social-development diasporic practice provides an opportunity to ruminate on the relationships among cultural identity, home, homeland orientation, and the conditions of diasporic emergence. As the following excerpt demonstrates, its celebration of developmentalism in homeland return is remarkable:

> Federico Macaranas, an economics professor at Manhattan College, said he would will be "going home" to the Philippines this month for the first time in 12 years to see how he and other Filipino-Americans could can help the new Government. . . .
>
> After all the victory celebrations for the end of the Marcos era, Filipino-Americans in New York and elsewhere are trying to translate joy into action. . . . Responding to President Corazon C. Aquino's "spirit of reconciliation," [groups] have welcomed the participation of all Filipino-Americans. Even former supporters of ex-President Ferdinand E. Marcos have begun to connect with this new movement, according to organizers. . . . "There's been such a groundswell of enthusiasm and readiness to help that we have to find ways to harness all this good will," Mr. Macaranas said. He and five other technicians have put together a project called Filipino-American International Transfer of Help, or Faith. The group plans to channel the expertise of Filipino-American professionals into the social and economic development of the Philippines. He stressed that the project had the support of a dozen key community groups but "would not be politicized."[16]

This article does not play on the pathos of its audience; there are no descriptions of starving children or desperate pleas for donations from its broad readership. Rather, it pinpoints how Filipino American immigrants and political exiles confer meaning to a post-Marcos era. What stands out is the article's characterization of and desires for collective connection or sense of a homeland devoid of the messiness and divisiveness of politics. While the post-Marcos era situates a sense of jubilance, neither the range of disastrous policies and modes of governance typically associated with the Marcos regime and martial law nor the reasons that the Ninoy Aquino Movement or any anti–martial law organization came to be make an appearance. We do not see the aftermath of the terror and violence of Marcos's martial law, the particular struggles for livelihood of landless rural peasants, or the upheavals of structural adjustment in the Philippines. We do not learn about the policies that intended to address the incredible national debt that was accumulated under Marcos. Rather, it focuses on how Filipino Americans can now redirect—or orient—their energies, sense of responsibility, and everyday lives toward the Philippines. The object of this news article is not the homeland or the Philippines itself but the diasporic homeland orientation of Filipino Americans.

Unlike anti–martial law organizing, in this article social-development efforts welcome all Filipinos into the fold: "Even former supporters of ex-President Ferdinand E. Marcos" are welcome to join. Filipino Americans can be assured that these efforts "would not be politicized," even though "going home" means helping the country's administration; the Corazon Aquino government (in "the spirit of reconciliation"); and despite the call to take part in social development projects being made by a political appointee, the new minister of natural resources. Celebrating the end of the Marcos era was framed as tantamount to Filipino America's ability and desire to unite and give back to the Philippines. The collective sigh of relief at the end of the Marcos era was accompanied by the notion that philanthropy and social development should fall outside politics and outside the realities of poverty and the afterlife of the Marcos regime. Phrases such as "translate joy into action," "a groundswell of enthusiasm and readiness to help," and "ways to harness all this good will" index the affective dimensions of diaspora giving, which must be understood as directly related to the antipolitics of this dominant diasporic homeland orientation.

Once assured that Filipino American community participation in social and economic development in the Philippines "would not be politicized," homeland orientation is reduced to heartfelt declarations of love for the homeland, erasing the material differences affecting homeland orientations and subsuming divisions related to the inequities produced by globalization. This unifying force of contemporary Filipino American diaspora is premised on a disavowal of politics and a disidentification with the multiple and sometimes oppositional frameworks of social transformation in the Philippines. Filipino American homeland orientation thus constitutes a site for the management of geopolitical and ideological anxieties in the production of diasporic space.[17] This relates to the diffusion of neoliberal logics that praise personal responsibility and the privatization of social needs and obscure how purportedly neutral economic policies work to perpetuate racial and gender hierarchies, including the racialization and feminization of "cheap" mobile Filipino labor. In this dominant homeland orientation, neither the diaspora nor Filipino America is situated within the natural realm of politics. This representation of unambiguous rupture between the Marcos era and the post-Marcos era, and the expressions of joy in the absence of politics, implicates a stable or essential Filipino identity, an authentic Filipinoness that had been temporarily buried beneath the divisions of social- and political-movement organizing during the Marcos dictatorship. To enter this new moment is to return to a state of unification. Rid of political divisiveness, Filipinos in the United States can come together through their collective homeland orientation.

I do not mean to suggest that to imagine counterhegemonic homeland orientations is to abandon philanthropy and social development within the realm of diaspora giving. The ideological conservatism of philanthropy and social development is not the sole concern of diaspora-giving critique, as the contexts are both broader and more specific. Developmentalism enables the hierarchal binding between the spaces and peoples of the Global North and Global South, between development agents and aid recipients, and between the cosmopolitan and the parochial. Filipino Americans navigate this terrain as both minoritized racialized subjects in the United States and as imagined or actual returnees to the Philippines. Triumphalist narratives of return by Filipino Americans valorize a diasporan's claim to the Philippines, a diasporic belonging legitimated through a generosity of spirit and the desire to give back to the homeland, and exemplify the immigrant's contributions to the United States. In a more specific context of U.S. racialized minority assimilationism and before philanthropic or social-development returns can occur, Filipino Americans must develop the work ethic and resources to fulfill their diasporic obligations as properly assimilated hyphenated Americans. For the abstract Filipino American returnee, these are assumptions of relative wealth and success and proper comportment that embody measures of economic and social assimilation to the national culture.

The agents of social development in the *New York Times* article cannot claim to be antipolitical; they are quite connected to politics and respond to the call of the Philippine state to help both impoverished Filipinos and the Philippine government. Rather, the antipolitics comes through in that neither the diaspora nor Filipino America is seen as operating within the realm of politics. The political Filipino subject is located in the Philippines, in the homeland, but not the home where the individual lives and works. It is a cultural identity and restoration of Filipinoness that gains its meaning through the refusal of an overt and structural politics of social change. It is a bifurcated diasporic subject who desires the restoration of a timeless Filipinoness that would enable an uncomplicated (nonpolitical) homeland return.

The representation of an idealized post-Marcos diasporic Filipino subject lay in marked contrast to the political reality of a post-Marcos homeland. Within the Philippines, there was not a collective sigh of relief, and Marcos's exile left no assurances of a clear path to social transformation from political and economic disarray. The ouster of Marcos after almost fourteen years of dictatorship and the rise of Corazon Aquino as heir to the presidency created an uncharted political situation for the country.[18] Political groups and bodies understood the opportunity to assert what they considered the political, economic, and social stakes of the immediate post-Marcos moment in the Philippines. The Corazon Aquino administration, with its moral authority to carry the legacy of her assassinated husband; the Catholic Church led by Cardinal Sin; the Philippine Left; the U.S. government, including its embassies in the Philippines; poor landless rural famers and urban laborers; international and foreign lender banks that were owed more than twenty billion dollars; Marcos loyalists already in political and civil-service positions; and the existing business, professional, and landed classes in the Philippines all had vested interests in the immediate post-Marcos moment. While those in power feared disruption of the status quo, rebuilding in the immediate post-Marcos era in the Philippines by organizations on the Left required serious attention to agrarian reform, strengthening labor amid efforts to revive production, renegotiating the incredible national debt, and making efforts toward poverty reduction following a kleptocratic dictatorship.[19] The contradictions of dominant Filipino American homeland orientation are apparent in Filipino America, in diaspora, and in the political reorganization of the Philippines that affected all classes of Filipinos.

Homeland Disorientations and Diaspora Studies

The precipitous rise of published academic work in the field of diaspora studies since the late 1980s produces little consensus on what the emergence of modern diasporas means for academic inquiry. In the inaugural issue of *Diaspora: A Journal of Transnational Studies*, for example, William Safran published an oft-cited effort to codify modern diasporas, enumerating the characteristics that "members of a genuine diaspora" would share "lest the term lose all meaning."[20] In Safran's schema, members of a genuine diaspora would maintain "a collective memory, vision, or myth about their original homeland" and "ethnocommunal consciousness or sense of solidarity" through a shared relationship to the homeland.[21] Lily Cho complicates Safran's theorization of diaspora and vehemently argues that "diaspora must be understood as a *condition of subjectivity*."[22] Cho writes, "Indeed, almost everyone seems to agree that diaspora, in its most basic sense, refers to a scattering of peoples who are nonetheless connected by a sense of a homeland, imaginary or otherwise. Beyond that, things get murkier."[23] While agreeing with Cho to approach diaspora as a condition of subjectivity, I would add that the way in which diasporic members are understood as "connected by a sense of a homeland, imaginary or otherwise," even before moving on to the "beyond" of Cho's overview of the term, is always contested.

To highlight the celebratory and triumphant nature of dominant narratives of diasporic return is to critique an unmediated, essentialized Filipinoness fulfilled or reanimated on return to the Philippine homeland. As Martin Manalansan writes, "Diasporic return is often portrayed as a romanticized end point, a moment characterized as either a rediscovery or a recovery of authenticity, a heroic and redemptive closure, or an idealized final destination of all diasporic odysseys and linear migratory movements."[24] This is the diasporic return I trace through dominant homeland orientations that contribute to the antipolitics of diaspora giving.

The surety and confidence of today's dominant homeland orientation normalizes developmentalist logics. To build a Filipino American diaspora-giving critique, I offer "disorientation" as a conceptual term to acknowledge the force of developmentalism in contemporary Filipino America diaspora and to introduce the disruption in which counterhegemonic practice may follow. In psychology and psychiatry, disorientation refers to a state marked by confusion, a condition characterized by a detachment from reality. Disorientation in psychology describes the inability to perceive oneself "correctly" in "time, place, situation (knowledge about one's current role and duties), and personal information (one's name, birth date, etc.)."[25] Psychologist Lucy Yardley emphasizes the relational aspect of this altered state as a feeling of uncertainty in one's environment: "Disorientation actually results from a combination of the individual, their behavior, and the context of their activities. . . . Someone who feels disoriented is, by definition, uncertain about his or her relationship to the environment, and disorientation can thus only arise in the course of some kind of interaction between individuals and their surroundings. Without accurate knowledge of orientation it is impossible properly to control posture or accomplish any kind of coordinated activity, and so disorientation can lead to staggering or falling."[26] A recent research report on disorientation published in *Cortex* states, "Most authors viewed disorientation as the result of an inability to store the information necessary to maintain an idea about the present. . . . More recent authors attributed disorientation to the combination of anterograde amnesia and retrograde amnesia: orientation to person was considered dependent on autobiographical memory while orientation to time and place was thought to depend on consolidation of new memories and on the capacity to update memory about time or location."[27]

This alteration of mental status is useful in theorizing disorientation in diaspora. To foster a homeland orientation suggests an element within collective identity that directs identification with the homeland and/or a spatial alignment to the homeland within collective identity. Naming a dominant homeland orientation prompts us to question the direction, singularity, and surety of homeland orientation. The surety with which Filipino American diasporic subjects proceed with giving projects emerges through affective attachments and collective memories of home in collaboration with developmentalist logics, assuring giving subjects that philanthropy and social development are the most significant ways to fulfill immigrant obligations and offer a better Philippine future. To suggest a collective homeland disorientation, then, is to intervene in the surety with which diaspora giving presses on and directs identification with the homeland. If collective diasporic identities involve the group's homeland orientation in time, place, and situation, then theorizing homeland disorientation and the complexity of home for diasporic subjects is an intervention in developmentalist logics. Dominant homeland orientation implies a recapture of a timeless Filipinoness outside politics, and a temporal disorientation is required to resituate the contingencies of diasporic subjectivities.

Homeland disorientation is not just about intervening in the surety of the goodness of philanthropy and social development. Homeland disorientation works to challenge the ways that development has ordered the world, including spaces of diaspora; the ways that diasporans integrate development as the raison d'être of diaspora; and the ways the developmentalist logics contribute to Filipino American subjectivity and discourse from outside and from within. There is no singular practice of homeland disorientation that would result in an ideal homeland reorientation, and disorientation itself does not amount to a new kind of thought and politics. Rather, a productive reorientation is renewed according to the exigencies of a particular moment in diasporic history. The force of dominant homeland orientations requires a disorientation to our way of understanding diasporic practice. It requires a reorientation to home.

Antidevelopmentalist Homeland Reorientation and Ninotchka Rosca's Political Discourse

Ninotchka Rosca is best known for her fiction and journalism. She has published seven books and received an American Book Award in 1993 for *Twice Blessed: A Novel*. Her activist life began as an anti–Vietnam War protester while a college student at the University of the Philippines in Diliman. As evidenced in my interviews with her, Rosca is very aware of the evolution of her social and political goals, narrating her political self through a reflection on the varied forms that her organizing efforts have taken: from her international solidarity organizing against the Vietnam War; to working with the anti–martial law movement; to cofounding the U.S.-based Gabriela Network (GABNet), a transnational solidarity women's organization working with the leftist and militant Gabriela women's organization in the Philippines; and to the politics that spur her current organization, Association of Filipinas, Feminists Fighting Imperialism, Re-feudalization, and Marginalization (AF3IRM). Rosca's political biography shows that her philosophy of organizing as a Filipina has followed broader political, economic, and cultural shifts. Her responses to those shifts are not ruptures from one type of commitment or moment to the next; Rosca has carried a consistent anger and critique of imperialist and patriarchal forces affecting Filipinos. Rather, they are permutations and rearrangements that respond to the bifurcation of Filipino labor. Rosca understands Filipino labor migrants as political and historical agents of social transformation, and tracing these political permutations and rearrangements reveals an important way to rethink the relationship between diaspora and home.

In a personal interview, Rosca described a shift in orientation to the Philippines that was fundamental to her ideological transformations. What began as a forced relocation to the United States to avoid political imprisonment in martial-law Philippines transformed into a politics of disorientation as a transnational Filipina. I asked Rosca her thoughts on how the label "political exile" has followed her while living, working, and organizing in the United States; how it may or may not capture her life; and what the possible consequences were of living under that label within Filipino America. In her response, Rosca identifies the spatial logic embedded in her particular diasporic existence: "This label 'political exile' is a judgment by itself, and it is also alienating, but at the same time it is also a recognition. It has a dual character. As a dialectical term, it has both good and bad aspects. I think because of that label, my first impulse in organizing was to organize for the Philippines."[28]

Rosca went on to describe how she brought the approach of organizing *for* the Philippines to her work with GABNet, an orientation that she later rethought. In many ways, GABNet had enormous success. Describes Rosca, "We were instrumental in organizing against U.S. military bases and raising awareness about the sex trafficking around them. We launched the first campaign on the comfort women issue . . . as well as on Asian American children abandoned by fathers. These campaigns led directly to the issue of mail-order brides and global sex trafficking, for which we practically had to invent a language, as almost no one was interested in it."[29] Earlier in the chapter, I describe the tensions between the CPP and the U.S.-based KDP over the KDP's insistence that issues affecting members as Filipino Americans have significant bearing on how they organize with the CPP as a U.S.-based solidarity organization for radical transformation in the Philippines. After martial law, Filipino America saw the deterioration of the solidarity movement with the Philippine Left during the struggle with the CPP. There was a time when GABNet was the sole remaining Philippine Left solidarity organization in the United States.

Organizing on behalf of Filipinos or on behalf of the Philippines has various implications for those in need of support, for Filipino American struggles, for homeland orientations, and for diaspora-giving critique. Says Rosca, "I had the sense [with GABNet] that there was something wrong with that approach. . . . I had the sense that there was something lacking in the approach. And it took a while for me to get to the point, 'Well, I am not an exile. I live here; I work here.'"[30] In short, bifurcation is problematic because it forces a singular orientation from multiply-placed diasporic subjects. Rosca's realization that "Well, I am not an exile. I live here; I work here" is, to impose my formulation, an identified moment of disorientation. Disoriented, Rosca honed her transnational Filipina political discourse, which she brings to her current work with the organization AF3IRM. "Our internationalism was best expressed, we felt, in dealing head-on with the material conditions in which we found ourselves—as our numbers were growing by leaps and bounds in the United States. We had to evolve—in one direction or another; and, following our impulse to contribute to the making of history, we chose collectively to become AF3IRM and engage fully with the situation here."[31] Rosca currently organizes around issues that infuse her diasporic, working, and activist commitments, saying, "That's why we [those working with AF3IRM] were very strict about what kind of issues we would take up: only those that had a direct link with the United States. There are issues [in the Philippines] like land for the landless. We can't take that up [as our primary organizing goal] because that is native feudalism that you have to work with. . . . That's why the slogan under which we founded AF3IRM was very simple—'From Nation to Home'—because it is not possible that our existence should be bifurcated. We have to bring it together—the economic, the political, the social—all of this. . . . We cannot be truncated. We cannot be bifurcated."[32]

Filipino American diaspora maintains a singular and unidirectional orientation toward the Philippines, and the social and political commitments of Filipino American diasporic subjects are split from economic lives as U.S.-based workers and from seeing themselves in relation to other workers or other U.S.-based communities struggling for self-determination or environmental justice. From an institutional perspective, this bifurcation, left unnamed, would contribute to a unilateral homeland orientation, structured by a compulsion to improve the conditions of women, poor people, and laborers in the Philippines but separated from the material conditions of home. Filipino Americans would be working on behalf of Filipinos in the Philippines, thus cutting their diasporic practice from the transnational forces that tie the United States to the Philippines; Filipinos in the United States to Filipinos elsewhere in the diaspora; and Filipinos in the United States to other racialized, sexualized, and exploited peoples in the places where those peoples live. This bifurcation also normalizes the antipolitics of dominant Filipino American diaspora giving despite the contradiction of U.S. and imperial racial formations.

Rosca's homeland reorientation helps us identify the hegemonic nationalist and depoliticized treatment of "home" and resists the normativizing impulses of diaspora and the transnational. The "political" in "the political exile" as engaged by Rosca is framed as a critique of the transnational political, economic, and social processes that would bifurcate a labor migrant's existence, split between her political life or social concerns in a homeland and economic life in the country where she lives. Rosca's political discourse contributes to a diaspora-giving critique that fosters broader possibilities for coalition and for home. This reorientation dislodges the romanticization of homeland—not only its timelessness but also its being the source for political, social, and giving commitments and responsibilities. If Filipino American diaspora-giving practices target widespread impoverishment or gendered violence, then a Filipinoness should encompass the connections between global capitalism and the reproduction of poverty in the Philippines, in the United States, and elsewhere.

Conclusion

Ninotchka Rosca states, "By affirming our right to be here, our right to fashion a life and a destiny for ourselves here, by affirming our right and duty to make history in the time and place of our lives . . . we defeat the original intent of martial law."[33] Rosca offers one alternative reimagining homeland orientation, a transnational Filipina/Filipino diasporic politics that privileges neither the homeland nor a singular home. This reorientation does not rely on the material and discursive power of America to claim belonging to the homeland through developmentalist logics. When she asserts that Filipinos affirm their right to "make history in the time and place of [their] lives," she suggests a diasporic homeland disorientation that counters dominant diasporic temporalities and spatialities. Kandice Chuh writes, "Positing the naturalness of the relationship between the native-born and the nation, such an ideology depends upon territoriality for coherence and, more specifically, upon a spatialized logic that holds as discreetly and naturally distinct 'here' and 'there.'"[34] How does Rosca defy a "nation-based territorial imagination" in diaspora giving?[35] Rosca holds transnationalism not as a description of bridging homeland politics and the realities of Filipino American lives but as "imperial forms and forces that endure" in migration, in legacies of deposed dictators, and in diasporic practice.[36]

3

Incorporating Dreams

Discourses of Poverty and Responsibility in Diaspora

Our main goal was to reverse the negative effect of the Philippine diaspora on the social and economic conditions of the country . . . by reviving the strong attachment of Filipinos abroad to the homeland so that they might be encouraged to go back, to give back, to reach out.

—DIOSDADO P. BANATAO, "Chairman's Message," in *Ayala Foundation USA Annual Report, 2007*

The pull quotes that draw the eye on the home page of the Philippine Development Foundation (PhilDev), a transnational nonprofit organization with offices in California and Metro Manila, greet readers with the boldest of missions: "Our mission is to eradicate poverty in the Philippines."[1] Here, the online audience begins to assess how PhilDev claims to accomplish this goal. Choosing phrases such as "removing obstacles" and "creating possibilities," which convey nonspecific but nonetheless evocative qualities, PhilDev presents itself as a proactive, resolute, and forward-thinking organization: "For future generations, having equal access to opportunities, we commit to eradicating poverty by removing obstacles to paths forward and creating possibilities where there were none."[2] This language invokes a possible future for poor people in the Philippines that makes it all but impossible for anyone to disagree. Referring to the Filipino American community as "the program's natural stakeholders," PhilDev markets its projects to Filipino Americans and utilizes their energies and expertise to create and support programming toward "sustainable and inclusive economic growth in the Philippines."[3]

As this book establishes, diaspora giving specifies the contexts and stakes of doing good and giving back, and PhilDev is the most visible and well-respected diaspora philanthropy organization in Filipino America. Its claim to "mobiliz[e] the Filipino diaspora to give back and support technology-driven innovations and entrepreneurship in the Philippines" resonates with Filipino America, and support for PhilDev is widespread.[4] PhilDev's claims are not necessarily controversial. However, the organization overlooks the structural causes of poverty and the reproduction of poverty within a global capitalist economy.

The organizational history of PhilDev sheds light on the limitations of its path forward. Its website states that the organization was launched in 2011, but the date does not tell its full origin story. In 2011, PhilDev requested a name change from the U.S. Internal Revenue Service. Formally a public charity registered as the Ayala Foundation USA (AF-USA), PhilDev began as the corporate social responsibility (CSR) arm of the Ayala Corporation (Ayala), the Philippines' oldest, largest, and most powerful corporate conglomerate, and the transnational extension of its Philippine-based Ayala Foundation.[5] Among its many philanthropic and social-development projects, the Ayala Foundation sponsors a youth leadership program in the Philippines, and it operates the Ayala Museum, the Filipinas Heritage Library, training and skills programs around the country, and until 2011, it operated AF-USA in California. The U.S.-based foundation did not pursue social-development projects in the United States; it existed as a mechanism for raising funds from Filipino America to support the Ayala Foundation's projects and its many partner nonprofit and charitable organizations in the Philippines.

Despite these lofty aims, it is curious that the most visible organization engaged in promoting Filipino American diaspora philanthropy prevents critical conversations about poverty and responsibility in diaspora. Figureheads of Ayala, the Ayala Foundation, AF-USA, and now PhilDev guide Filipino American diaspora-giving practice in significant measure. Their enormous efforts in shaping diasporic philanthropic practice and history of contributing to social-development conversations at high levels within the global community have created a vast public record of the Ayala Foundation's framework of social transformation.

The current figureheads of Ayala—brothers Jaime Augusto Zobel de Ayala II and Fernando Zobel de Ayala—were integral in institutionalizing CSR practice in the Philippines.[6] In an interview published in 2003, Jaime Augusto describes his belief that philanthropy and CSR are necessary for corporations to build trust with the communities they serve:

> Philanthropy is a natural impulse of people to adjust to the social development needs of their environment. In developing countries like the Philippines, where at least a third of our people live below the poverty line, individual and corporate philanthropy are critical in complementing the limited budget of government in addressing the basic needs of the disadvantaged. They are necessities in the struggle for social justice, for true equality, and for social and economic development. Indeed, I believe that corporate social responsibility is a strategic management tool that all companies must learn to integrate into their operations if they are to develop a sustainable model of "trust" with the many communities they serve.[7]

Jaime Augusto positions corporate philanthropy as a necessary complement to governmental social welfare efforts. Corporations and corporate philanthropy, he argues, are not a hindrance but integral to the fight for social justice and "true equality."

More recently, the Asia Philanthropy Circle profiled Jaime Augusto's brother, Fernando, as one of the twenty-five most "impactful philanthropists" in the Association of Southeast Asian Nations (ASEAN). The profile included interview snippets with Fernando, a key corporate player in Southeast Asia, on his philosophy of social responsibility. The Asia Philanthropy Circle writers echoed the language of progressive politics that Jaime Augusto used in 2003, characterizing the relationship between Ayala's business ventures and philanthropy as a "palpable synergy."[8] The writers heralded Ayala's dual commitment to profit and "progressive social impact": "With their guidance, the Ayala brand has bred a palpable synergy between the corporate and philanthropic arms to channel the resources of both ends into progressive social impact. The journey of the Ayala brand from philanthropy to CSR to more active and meaningful engagement with society's needs relates to its inclusive business mandate: Ensuring that business is not a problem but rather, a solution to society's problems."[9] Similar to Jaime Augusto's insistence that corporate philanthropy complements the government's mandate to address its population's basic needs, Fernando's profiler's insistence that "business is not a problem but rather, a solution to society's problems" naturalizes the benevolence of capitalism in general and disregards the harmful tendencies of the market. This imagining excises the devastating side effects of existing markets, which forces an examination of the Ayalas' role in shaping the discourse of poverty in the Philippines.

If the Ayala foundations were not so influential and Ayala not a center of economic power in the Philippines, it would be tempting to dismiss Jaime Augusto and Fernando's solutions to widespread poverty in the Philippines as simply self-serving or cynical, another marketing ploy that just happens to name the Filipino diaspora as a tool for social development. However, a senior fellow at the John F. Kennedy School of Government cites Ayala as one of the most internationally celebrated examples of good corporate citizenship.[10] AF-USA was held as a model for diaspora philanthropy—not just for Filipinos but for all new diasporic populations. Numerous international organizations have invited the former president of the Ayala Foundation and the AF-USA, Victoria Garchitorena, to make presentations on the foundations' approach to diaspora philanthropy.[11] Garchitorena was a featured speaker for two separate United Nations–sponsored conferences as an expert on diaspora philanthropy and was the lead researcher for a case study on the Philippines that examined the relationship between diaspora and development.[12] Their efforts model an international turn to diasporans as new development actors.

To give a sense of its economic enormity, the Ayala group of companies, the third-largest conglomerate in the Philippines, reached market capitalization of ₱492.3 billion (Philippine pesos) in the Philippine Stock Exchange at the end of 2019.[13] That year, its full-year earnings reached ₱35.5 billion, and its total assets amounted to ₱1.3 trillion.[14] Ayala is a publicly traded, family holding company, and it owns Bank of the Philippine Islands, the country's largest and most profitable bank, and holds interests in Globe Telecom, a major Philippine telecommunications company; the Manila Water Company, the Ayala Insurance Holdings Corporation; and contract assembly, electronics manufacturing, export processing, air charter service, food and agribusiness, and automotive companies. Ayala owns Ayala Land, Inc., which includes hotels, real estate development, management companies, and the Ayala Malls, one of the country's largest shopping mall chains. Its companies extend internationally in such places as Hong Kong, Japan, Malaysia, Australia, Singapore, Macau, Thailand, Indonesia, and the United States and contributes to areas such as property development, investment holding, trading, and fund management. Its presence in the Philippines, seen through advertising, university endowments, development partnerships, newspaper and magazine articles, political connections, public goods projects, and aristocratic Spanish-era family largesse, is almost without peer.[15]

Ayala's market capitalization and dominance in the Philippine economy mean that PhilDev cannot account for, and does not challenge, the ways that the rich are getting richer and does not address the resultant poverty. Its "meaningful engagement with society's needs" is a framework of social transformation that accepts extreme levels of inequality. The contrast between corporate promises to deliver the solution to poverty in the Philippines and the rate at which Ayala has been able to generate profit is stark. In 2006, when Jaime Zobel de Ayala Sr. was still the patriarch of the family business, before handing over operations to his two sons, he was worth $2 billion according to *Forbes*.[16] In 2020, the same publication lists his wealth at $3.6 billion (and the Ayala corporate conglomerate's revenue at $3.9 billion), an 80 percent increase in wealth from 2006.[17]

The Ayala foundations presume that this degree of wealth is not at all incompatible with solutions to poverty. Moreover, as architects of diaspora philanthropy, their solution to poverty extends to the diasporic politics produced through Filipino America's acceptance of the foundations' guidance and assurance that theirs is a legitimate voice in dealing with suffering and precarity in the Philippines. As a result, poverty is individualized and neoliberal logics are systematically reproduced.

I read the self-representation of the Ayala Foundation, AF-USA, and PhilDev and their engagements with diaspora philanthropy through organization publications and websites; public statements by the presidents, chairmen, and directors regarding the goals and vision of the foundations; my interviews with directors and consultants; and my participation in conferences and workshops supported by the Ayala foundations. Rather than evaluate the success or failure in meeting their stated goals through their various social-development projects and partnerships, which is outside the scope of this project, this chapter contextualizes the ideological work performed by the corporate foundations as they claim for themselves a prominent place in the world of diaspora philanthropy. The chapter then considers the material implications of neoliberal capitalist ideals and practices in Filipino American diaspora giving. Just as consciously as Ayala contributes to the discourse on diaspora philanthropy, so should a diaspora-giving critique examine the premises on which it stakes its claims. Through this analysis the chapter intervenes in dominant poverty discourse and questions the way it shapes diaspora and diasporic belonging. This effort points to the relationship between poverty and responsibility, suggesting alternative diaspora-giving imaginings.

Corporate-Diasporic Social Responsibility

Members of the Ayala clan influenced the growth of CSR in the Philippines, and their diaspora philanthropy philosophies and organizations emerged from this commitment. Historically in the West, CSR programs came about in response to critiques of corporate capitalism in the 1960s and 1970s, critiques that called for a reimagining of corporate regulation and the corporation's social duties and obligations.[18] As Joshua Barkan covers in his genealogy of the corporation, "Corporate power has always been articulated within the context of responsibility. Discourses of responsibility, citizenship, and commitments to serve public welfare (in however strange or dreadful ways) are the very ontological root of the corporation and its legal justifications for existence. Corporations and their advocates have long made the legal argument . . . that their exceptional status is warranted because they carry the responsibilities of serving society and public welfare."[19] The legal existence of corporations hinged on the threat that they pose to public welfare and an acknowledgment of their social responsibilities in exchange for the protected right of their incorporation. Corporations bear social responsibility for the dangers and potential for vast inequality they pose in their legal existence. Because of the familiar ways that corporations can co-opt and commoditize the language of community, social justice, and "true equality," as seen in the Ayalas' statements, the question should not be about how to make corporations take responsibility for social welfare or social development but rather how to imagine alternative approaches to institutionalizing social responsibility. This is manifest in examinations of poverty discourse and the insistence that structural causes of injustice be addressed in the reproduction of poverty within a global capitalist system. At the very least, the realm of Filipino American diaspora giving must not foreclose conversations about the imposition of poverty and injustice.

The 1990s and 2000s mark the international turn to "diaspora philanthropy," and the Ayalas were an integral part of this move in the Philippines. Their extended CSR efforts led them to incorporate Filipino Americans and the Filipino diaspora as additional assemblages among their various stakeholders, recognized units of "Ayala's ecosystem" and corporate vision.[20] After the original incorporation of the Ayala Foundation USA in 2000, Fernando called on Filipino America to help him "open a new chapter in the story of Filipino-Americans," saying, "I firmly believe Filipinos in America, as well as those who have succeeded in other countries, have much to contribute to the dynamic social development landscape back home. . . . We solicit your assistance as a way for you to give back effectively to the communities, the provinces and the country that nurtured you."[21] His "new chapter in the story of Filipino-Americans" resonates with the question of how Filipino Americans enter Filipino American diasporic history addressed in Chapter 2. Here, Fernando offers Filipino Americans the opportunity to enter diasporic history through support for Ayala's vision of social transformation. Fernando and the Ayala Foundation want Filipino Americans to help shoulder the responsibility for social development in the Philippines, not simply because they left the Philippines for life in the United States or because Filipino Americans are directly guilty of exacerbating poverty in the Philippines but because the country nurtured them, setting them up for their future success. Diaspora philanthropy organizations bring a sense of collective responsibility to what it means to be Filipino in diaspora, and the culture to which diasporic organizations contribute can be understood as a site of struggle where dominant discourses of poverty and responsibility can be either secured or contested. I understand these as the stakes of diaspora giving today.[22]

Poverty discourses that are unable to address capitalism's role in generating inequality and exploitation mask the structural forces that reproduce poverty. As addressed in the introduction to this book, the charitable uplift of Filipinos legitimized large-scale projects of development, including American colonization in the Philippines, which laid the foundation for neocolonialism and the export of Filipino labor. Structural adjustment programs forced on developing countries by the World Bank and IMF exacerbated the gulf between the impoverished and the wealthy within countries such as the Philippines, as their imperatives prioritized economic development and integration into the global economic order. The Marcos regime famously built up the country's debt to enrich its family and cronies, leaving the country financially vulnerable and unable to address poverty with public expenditures. Colonial control of resources and industries; neocolonial political-economic relations; myopic official development projects, including the deregulation of national industries; and dictatorial greed have contributed to poverty and the vulnerability of the impoverished. However, for corporate foundations, the profit directive isolates the discussion of poverty away from the creation of poverty, and the relationship between extreme poverty and wealth, and toward the individual.[23]

When poverty is individualized, the collective sense of belonging and collective obligation often run counter to notions of injustice,[24] and when organizations such as PhilDev and AF-USA identify injustice in explanations for poverty, they ascribe a level of responsibility to the poor themselves.[25] Analyses of structural causes of poverty lead to ideas of the social that are not accounted for in the corporate sense of responsibility. In the posthumously published *Responsibility for Justice*, political theorist Iris Marion Young writes, "To judge a circumstance unjust implies that we understand it at least partly as humanly caused, and entails the claim that something should be done to rectify it. On the other hand, when the injustice is structural, there is no clear culprit to blame and therefore no agent clearly liable for rectification."[26] Poverty in the Philippines cannot be pinned on any one body. It is not a productive project to assign direct liability to

Ayala for the poverty of tens of millions Filipinos in the Philippines. However, we must be aware of the reality of diverting attention from structural critique in diaspora giving.

It has been made abundantly clear that Ayala has shaped what Filipino American diaspora stands for and how Filipino Americans enter diasporic history as agents of social transformation. Ayala is an almost untouchable target for criticism in certain parts of Filipino America, which is due in large part to its commitments to social development and its reputation for choosing to remain outside the inner circles of Philippine political corruption. Even proposing a critical study of poverty discourse in the Filipino American diaspora that might implicate Ayala led to some tense moments for me. For example, at one public event following the presentation of my work, a fellow academic and well-known anti–martial law organizer in the United States stood up and waved her finger. She rebuked my efforts, saying in agitation, "How can you critique the Ayala Foundation USA? We all give to the Ayalas. They bring internet to schools in the Philippines. Do you not support bringing internet to those schools?" Clearly, I had touched a nerve.

The strength of this person's defense of AF-USA and the Ayalas speaks to certain social norms in diaspora. From 2000 to 2010, AF-USA raised money from Filipino America and gained the support of Filipino American associations and organizations for their social-development projects in the Philippines. They partnered with national organizations, well-established Filipino American philanthropists, and government officials and consulate offices in the United States.[27] Many Filipino Americans saw AF-USA as the principal mediator for giving back to the Philippines, and to those Filipino Americans it was beyond reproach. The Ayala Foundation changed the name of AF-USA to PhilDev in 2010, and it became an independent organization in 2011. The Ayala Foundation had considered changing the Ayala Foundation USA name to PhilDev or something similar since at least 2005 to distance itself from the Ayala corporate moniker, hoping to quell criticism that the foundation was merely an extension of the corporation's budgets and business goals.[28] In late 2011, the Ayala Foundation in the Philippines divested from PhilDev so that PhilDev was no longer listed as a part of Ayala's CSR initiatives, the brothers Zobel de Ayala were no longer listed as founders of PhilDev, and PhilDev no longer primarily advocated for the Ayala Foundation's signature projects in the Philippines. However, PhilDev's status in Filipino America is indebted to its organizational history as a project of CSR, and its proposed solutions to poverty remain consistent with Ayala's.

Filipino America fosters an enlarged identity that connects hometown, regional, or national commitments to new identities as philanthropists, humanitarians, benefactors, and activists. While transnational giving is not new, the last few decades have seen an explosion of Filipino American organizations, associations, and foundations that are designed to aid the Philippines. From the mutual aid societies of early Filipino immigrants to the United States, the post-1965 immigrant Filipino Americans have organized themselves into *thousands* of associations as well as professional, alumni, and activity groups in every state in the nation. Following the swell of immigration of Filipino medical professionals in the late 1960s and 1970s, Filipino American doctors and nurses devote themselves to medical missions in the Philippines, demonstrating that homeland was never left completely behind. In the past three decades in particular, Filipino Americans have created new organizations and foundations for the specific purpose of transnational development and partnership with communities in the Philippines. Associations that originally banded together for social activities and mutual aid among Filipino Americans have redirected their emphasis to doing what they can to raise money from the Filipino American community to finance projects benefiting homeland communities.

The economic position of many middle-class, post-1965 professionals; the international neoliberal policies that redirect responsibility for social welfare away from the state; and the increased ease of travel to and communication with the Philippines have all intersected to enliven today's field of Filipino American diaspora-giving organizations. The increasing numbers of these organizations and the frequent conferences and symposia being held by their leaders in the Philippines and Filipino America underline the importance of studying the role of giving in the production of diasporic identities and transnational community formations.

Globalization has irreversibly altered the ways that collectivities such as diasporas and nations address social-economic relations and political representation. Even as transnationalism produces new community formations and nationalisms, the international remains divided into geopolitical territories in unequal relationships of power.[29] Therefore, globalization requires a reframing of the space of social demands and "the structural causes of many injustices in a globalizing world" that differentially affect the space of, within, and between the United States and the Philippines.[30] Financial markets, multinational corporations, export processing zones, and the larger "governance structures of the global economy" exceed the geopolitical boundaries of the nation-state.[31] A critical politics of diaspora giving must address not only the spatial relationships of diaspora but also the spatial relationships regarding organized development and economic redistribution. Particular Filipino American diaspora-giving practices reflect new spaces of belonging and deflect attention from the spatialization of injustice. Giving and return are inexorably linked for migrants, and AF-USA and PhilDev work to unite Filipino America through their own systems of transfer and aid. CSR programs, or the private sector's response to the "'externalities' associated with economic globalization," such as unsustainably low wages and unhealthy working conditions, are "presented as a way to balance the interests of business and society *without* expanding government intervention in the global market place."[32]

The logics that sustain Ayala's position in the Philippine political economy and the Philippines' role in the global economy are transmitted by their discourse on diaspora philanthropy. Diosdado P. Banatao is the current chairman of PhilDev and the former chair of AF-USA's board of directors. In the AF-USA 2008 annual report, Banatao writes, "Undeterred by all the challenges we face, we continue to dream of a world where Filipinos, wherever they are, are bound together by their common desire to effect positive change in the Philippines."[33] The irony of this statement being delivered by a representative of the country's largest corporate foundation on behalf of one the country's richest business families is thick, particularly when it is intended to understand how dreams and hopes are produced through, and as a supplement to, Ayala's position in the political economy of the Philippines. Dreams for a better Philippines are shaped through their vision of social transformation and human need. Ayala's use of a CSR and the subsequent organization of its corporate foundations are also forms of imagining, of a social order in which the externalities of global industry neither contradict its role in diaspora philanthropy nor impede the freedom for profit making. The fantasy of CSR regulates the Ayala-produced mode of giving, which appropriates desires for return to a Philippine homeland.

My use of imagining and fantasy here are indebted to the critical work of Neferti Xina M. Tadiar. In *Fantasy-Production*, Tadiar argues that "dreams are the concrete work of imagination" and that "imagination, as culturally organized social practice, is an intrinsic, constitutive part of political economy":[34]

> Capitalism and state rule, and not only nationalism, are suffused with imagination. Unless we think that political and economic structures are the sole invention of those in power, it makes important sense to see the social force of imagination at work in these "structural realities" before its expression in recent, more visible "culturalist" forms such as ethnic nationalism and the active construction of new diasporic identities through electronic media.[35]

In accordance with Tadiar, Ayala's evocations of diaspora philanthropy cannot be understood as distinct or separate from the fantasy of the free world in which the Philippines participates in its export of racialized, sexualized, and gendered Filipino bodies as labor or from the regimes of accumulation and standards of free trade, development, and corporate citizenship in which Ayala participates. To understand Ayala's desires—harkening back to Banatao's statement—as universal, as every Filipino's wish for a Philippines with less hunger and poverty, is to ignore the extent that such dreams "fuel and further the logics of the dominant global order."[36] Furthermore, even the initial clause of Banatao's statement, that Ayala is "undeterred by all the challenges we face," raises crucial questions for diaspora giving. To not be deterred represents a fantasy of corporate philanthropy—"the shared ground upon which the actions and identities of its participants are predicated," to again borrow from Tadiar—and how it seeks to organize the space of diaspora and homeland.[37]

International NGOs and multilateral organizations recognize the Ayala Foundation as a leader in promoting the ideals of CSR and for developing an international model for diaspora philanthropy. As Ayala defends its status in the Philippine political economy, the diasporic dreams of the Ayala Foundation obscure the extent to which its very existence depends on the protection and elaboration of global capitalism. Ayala has significantly influenced the Philippine economy. Notably, it grew during the Corazon Aquino presidential administration, which coincided with the height of neoliberal structural-adjustment polities. The Ayala Group was central in implementing the strategy to develop export processing zones for semiconductors and agribusiness, which the government pursued in continuance of the guidelines of neoliberal multilateral lending agencies, contributing to the international division of labor and the racialization and feminization of cheap Filipino labor.[38] Part of the power of large corporate foundations is that they control or contain more radical demands than can be encapsulated, for example, by the Ayala Foundation's list of "legitimate organizations" for the Filipino American market. These foundations present themselves as the solution to systemic inequalities and unequal access to resources. The resulting program of diaspora philanthropy, while serving a range of populations with often dire and immediate needs, functions to contain anticapitalist threats in the Philippines and promotes a Filipino American diaspora that negates the possibility of addressing inequalities.

Corporate Citizenship and Diasporic Belonging

The institutionalization and rise of transnational CSR programs in the Philippines provide an opportunity to examine how today's giving and philanthropic practices are structured by global capital and how global capital and the logics of neoliberalism infuse diaspora formation, the interplay of diaspora-homeland-market, and the framing and politics of Filipino American diaspora giving. Corporate philanthropy is a very specific form of giving; Philippine-based corporations put calls to Filipinos in the United States to help the motherland—and is leaving a significant mark on Filipino American communities. Poverty and hunger are widespread in the Philippines, and many Filipino Americans have the desire and resources to help, but the methods through which poverty and hunger are addressed thwart critical discussions of the contradictions of globalization, transnational capitalism, and responsibility and contribute to the dehistoricization of poverty and development. Such sentiments abet neoliberalism; dominant forms of giving back are understood as separate from processes of commodification or as a purer alternative to the market. As the actions of AF-USA, which is inextricably linked to the Ayala corporation, demonstrate, nonprofits are not necessarily outside capitalism or anticapitalistic in their nature.[39] Moreover, the resulting diaspora philanthropy deployed by Ayala "lowers the consciousness" of the material relations that enable the accumulation of wealth experienced by the Ayala family.[40]

CSR's ability to articulate moral concerns alongside profit-oriented business goals produces a difficult terrain to navigate. The Ayala Foundation's goals are informed by its commitment to community, the public, and business ethics. Jaime Augusto states:

> We all pay for poverty and unemployment and illiteracy. If a large percentage of society falls into a disadvantaged class, investors will find it hard to source skilled and alert workers; manufacturers will have a limited market for their products; criminality will scare away foreign investments, and internal migrants to limited areas of opportunities will strain basic services and lead to urban blight. Under these conditions, no country can move forward economically and sustain development. . . . It therefore makes business sense for corporations to complement the efforts of government in contributing to social development.[41]

Elsewhere, he elaborates on his view of a comfortable alliance between social development and profit:

> We have always realized that there is a strong link between broad social development and the potential for long-term corporate profitability. . . . Investors are increasingly sophisticated nowadays and we believe that they are acutely aware that CSR/corporate citizenship and the fortunes of companies in the private sector are inextricably linked, especially in emerging or developing markets such as the Philippines. This is because

> broad social development will effectively be able to expand the current market boundaries that companies in emerging markets face, therefore increasing the size of the pie in the long term.[42]

Jaime Augusto strips the reality of poverty of everything except its potential to cause the business sector loss in profits and foreign investment. While those who are actually poor may "pay for" it through lack of housing, water, or education, Jaime Augusto casts the true victims of poverty as the business and manufacturing sectors. As a result, to again borrow from Tadiar, "the moral concern for Filipino society translates into an economic concern for its competitive advancement."[43]

The former development specialist for the Ayala Foundation, Mariel Q. de Jesus, encourages the Philippine public to trust Ayala's fundamental morality:

> While some critique [CSR] as mere marketing or public relations ploys, some companies have taken CSR to heart, incorporating the principles of CSR into their corporate mission and values, and finding ways to integrate these into their business operations. Some corporations take the long-term view when it comes to CSR. Recognizing that it takes time for investments in social development to bear fruit, these companies bank on the moral bottom line: doing good because it's the right thing to do.[44]

CSR programs are produced as a sign of the morality of the economic order. Doing good because it is right generates a rhetorical and moral tautology that refuses the connection between doing good and the historical extent and production of poverty and inequality. While Jaime Augusto links the Philippines' need for social development to CSR "and the fortunes of companies in the private sector," he does so with an eye toward creating new markets among the poor and disregards the realities of poverty. The rhetoric of Ayala celebrates the corporation's ability to excel financially, producing billions in wealth for a few, and simultaneously to deliver the country from underdevelopment. As described on its website, "Anchored on values of integrity, long-term vision, empowering leadership, and with a strong commitment to national development, Ayala fulfills its mission to ensure long-term profitability and value creation."[45] Such rhetoric mirrors what Jean Comaroff and John L. Comaroff describe as triumphant or "millennial capitalism": "We seek . . . to draw attention to, to interrogate, the distinctly pragmatic qualities of the messianic, millennial capitalism of the moment: a capitalism that presents itself as a gospel of salvation; a capitalism that, if rightly harnessed, is invested with the capacity wholly to transform the universe of the marginalized and disempowered."[46] The former president of the Ayala Foundation and AF-USA, Victoria Garchitorena, echoes this sentiment: "AF-USA will continue to serve as a conduit between Filipinos in the U.S. and in the Philippines. We urge you to continue helping uplift the lives of the underprivileged, even beyond times of calamity. For as long as there is an individual deprived of his or her rights, there will always be work for us to do."[47] Participation in millennial capitalism positions the Ayala Foundation as the savior of the poor and the voice of diaspora.

Jaime Augusto, also writing on Ayala's messianic facilities, states:

> The economic sources of philanthropic wealth have likewise changed from, say, railroads, mines, steel mills, car production, explosives or war material in the 20th century, to software, food production, finance, energy, shipping, retailing or real estate in the 21st century. But the ethical standards and moral expectations governing the acquisition of wealth backing philanthropies are now demanding stringent adherence to the highest levels of good governance. Corporate social responsibility emerged and flourished as an idea that encompasses philanthropy but includes the moral purposes that businesses serve on the way to generating the profits that will eventually finance philanthropic giving. Business, more than ever, is expected to operate ethically in the market.[48]

Jaime Augusto refers to wealth as "philanthropic wealth," and his rhetoric implies that his multinational corporation's drive for profits and new markets will help the poor. He argues that in this post-Fordist economy, the social contract has changed such that successful businesses must, on account of their success, already be inherently moral and beyond reproach. Correspondingly, Fernando's speech to the Philippine Advertising Congress describes what Ayala has to offer corporations of the future:

> We need to fundamentally reorient this economic paradigm towards a more "responsible and enlightened form of capitalism," one that seeks long-term sustainability and balance, one that uses the mechanisms of the free market, but recognizes the needs of the broader community. If we don't, I'm afraid we will continue on a path that leads to more frequent natural disasters and the resulting toll on human suffering and poverty. . . . This is capitalism that uses market forces to address the needs of the poor, those at the base of the economic pyramid, who in the past were not considered a profitable market. This is capitalism that looks at greening the supply chain, that minimizes environmental footprint, that seeks more efficient use of natural resources and replaces those it has used.[49]

Fernando communicates the anxieties of a rampant capitalism that contributes to natural disasters and human suffering. He addresses unenlightened capitalism's contribution to the suffering of the poor by such natural disasters. However, he cannot link even unenlightened capitalism to the production and perpetuation of poverty. His enlightened capitalism uses the same market forces that would lead unenlightened business to exacerbate suffering but, for the enlightened, toward meeting the needs of the poor. CSR, therefore, can transform suffering into the satisfaction of needs. This is the purported triumph of enlightened capitalism.[50]

In a special issue of *International Affairs* on CSR, coeditor Michael Blowfield makes the case for a more critical perspective of CSR and how it frames the poor and marginalized in developing countries: "The most clearly apparent limitations to the approaches typical of contemporary CSR relate to the fundamental values and tenets of the capitalist enterprise," to which Blowfield includes the right to make a profit, "the commoditization of things including labour," and "the privileging of companies as citizens and moral entities." "It is surprising," he continues, "that so little is made of these basic values in the supposedly values-oriented world of CSR."[51]

The Ayala Foundation began its articulation of development, CSR, philanthropy, and the Filipino American diaspora after it commissioned a study that described the promise of this potential market. In 2003, AF-USA contracted consultant J. Robbie Fabian to perform a pre-marketing study of Filipino American donors and their philanthropic patterns, inclinations, and interests. Fabian presented in his report an analysis of "the current philanthropic involvement and practices of Filipino Americans in the United States [and] their linkages with and perceptions of nonprofit causes and non-governmental organizations (NGOs) working directly in the Philippines."[52] He continues with the self-description of the study:

> Ayala Foundation USA was conceived and developed by the Ayala Corporation as an initiative to encourage Filipino American philanthropic giving directly to Philippine causes, as a strategy to bolster the nonprofit sector of the country. . . . The incorporation of the Ayala Foundation USA was based in part on the assumption that Filipino American donors markets are potential sources of major funding for Philippines causes. . . . We assume that the potential of the Filipino American market to support Philippine causes is not fully tapped due to the lack of comprehensive fundraising strategies and campaigns in the United States.[53]

The Ayala Foundation creates the "truth" of the Filipino American market and, therefore, the extent of diaspora philanthropy.[54] Its mobilization of diaspora philanthropy transforms Filipino Americans into a market. As is made clear by Fabian, the Ayala Foundation pursues the Filipino American market in efforts "to bolster the nonprofit sector" of the Philippines. The nonprofit sector, with its safety mechanisms and its nominal and effective relationship to the profit industry, is not the only space for social change in the Philippines or elsewhere, although it is represented as such. Moreover, this nonprofit sector is anointed by the state, multilateral institutions, and

CSR programs such as the Ayala Foundation as the legitimate arbiters of development, obscuring other forms and demands for social transformation, particularly given the Ayala Foundation's role in identifying what are considered legitimate causes and organizations for its Filipino American market.

Even though Ayala describes itself as having a platform of systemic change toward the alleviation of poverty in the Philippines, CSR programs came about in response—and as an alternative—to political activism and international protests of the 1960s and 1970s. Historically, business leaders created CSR as a business paradigm to build trust for their companies in the face of third-world organizing and emerging radicalism. Consider, for example, the following description of the history of CSR in the Philippines:

> Discontent in the countryside and in factories led to massive protest demonstrations that came to be known as the riotous period of "First Quarter Storm" [in the Philippines].[55] As businessmen began to witness demonstrations within the financial district where they worked, some progressive leaders began to reassess the role played by business in the country's development. Their conclusion was that while business had been supporting various charitable activities on a sporadic, fragmented and uncoordinated basis, there was a growing need for organized, professional and continuing assistance.[56]

As a direct result of radical social agitation, business leaders developed and extended their CSR programs to funnel and address discontent through organized, formal development and corporate philanthropy. These programs continue attempts to hold sway over political activism, particularly through self-initiated sustainability programs, so that advocacy groups will not organize in the political arena.[57] The narrative of social transformation offered to Filipino Americans through diaspora philanthropy redirects discontent and funnels the emotions and attachments enlivened by diasporic desires toward marketized world making.

Ayala naturalizes the corporate sense of responsibility, removes it from its history, and presents a clearly business-oriented solution to poverty. As stated by Jaime Augusto, "CSR is a *natural impulse* of people to adjust to the social development needs of their environment. . . . I am proud of all the projects that Ayala Foundation has undertaken. They have always looked for innovative solutions to the problems of poverty through effective and efficient programs."[58] However, Ayala's contributions to diaspora philanthropy are not inevitable; they are a strategic incorporation of marketized values and identities. CSR, as the business influence of development, is multiply implicated in the neoliberalization of donor subjects.[59] The hegemony of neoliberal common sense concerning the power and the good of the market has controlled public debate for decades. The questions asked about the possibilities of corporate-sponsored diaspora philanthropy, which are also the possibilities of Filipino American diaspora subjectivities in the corporate sense of responsibility, are limited by the extent to which neoliberal thought has set the terms of the debate.

Filipino America: "Your Logical Market"

At its inception, the Ayala Foundation depended on large grants from external sponsors such as the Ford Foundation in addition to the portion of its operating money received from Ayala. Beginning in the post–cold war 1990s, the directors and managers of the Ayala Foundation noticed a decrease in funding from external sponsors and state-sponsored development agencies, particularly from the United States, Canada, and Japan. To maintain support for its projects and for NGOs in the Philippines, the Ayala Foundation turned its energies toward Filipino America. As an Ayala Foundation manager, Tony Acoba, revealed in an interview:

> The Ayala Foundation USA was created in 2000 mainly because in [the] Ayala Foundation, we realized that the money that we get for social-development activities from the different funding agencies is getting smaller every year, so we thought that it would be good to tap the Filipino Americans. Because, I think, the estimate is about sixty percent or more of the remittance comes from the U.S., the U.S. becomes your logical market for looking for funds. Previously, most NGOs in the Philippines would only depend on writing and submitting

> proposals to these funding agencies, but now that [funding has been] transferred to other countries, we had to find a better way of mobilizing funds for social development.[60]

This larger international shift would play an important role in how the Ayala Foundation figured Filipino Americans and the Filipino diaspora into its social-development projects in the Philippines.

Initially, AF-USA intended to raise money from within Filipino America to benefit a general development fund that it would control and disperse to Philippine-based social-development projects and NGOs. The foundation had hoped, said Acoba, that Filipino Americans "would just give, would entrust their money to the foundation and . . . assume that we would give it to certain development needs, the greatest needs of our country." As the foundation discovered through experience with donors and through its own research with Filipino American–targeted focus groups, most Filipino American donors wanted, instead, to have more control and direct their gifts to particular organizations and be able to attach a specific organization or project name to their monetary donations. As a result, the Ayala Foundation began to foster direct and more sustained relationships with nonprofit organizations and NGOs in the Philippines that the foundation deemed "worthy of public support." It marketed these organizations to the Filipino American donor pool.[61] Filipino American donors could then choose their recipients through a list of organizations with projects approved and monitored by the Ayala Foundation in the Philippines.

NGOs and nonprofit organizations are "imagined to be expressions of community," describes Miranda Joseph in *Against the Romance of Community*, proposing that "both the rhetorical invocation of community and the social relationships that are discursively articulated as community are imbricated in capitalism," prompting an argument "against the idealization of community as a utopian state of human relatedness."[62] The relationship between NGOs and this idea of community appears in this current case study in two ways: in the production of the Philippine homeland and of the Filipino American diaspora. During the time of its operation, the NGOs partnered by and listed on the AF-USA website are, collectively, AF-USA's expression of the imagined community of the Philippine nation, the imagined homeland of the diaspora. The Ayala Foundation portrays the Philippine national community through its assemblage of NGOs in the Philippines that are worthy of Filipino American support or as the sanctioned routes toward diaspora-sponsored national development. It claims this responsibility and legitimizes its role in leading a diaspora philanthropy movement in large part through the financial successes and economic vision of its parent company, shaping and defining the giving opportunities available to the Filipino American diaspora.

The community invoked by the Ayala Foundation's promise of social responsibility extends to Filipinos in America as partners in national development. This institutionalization of diaspora philanthropy contains the Filipino American diaspora's desire to engage social inequality and labor exploitation in the Philippines. In his history of CSR initiatives, James Rowe argues "that the primary reason for business's trenchant interest in corporate codes is that they are an effective means of quelling popular discontent with corporate power and the political change that discontent might impel."[63] The Ayala Foundation's extensive commitments to institutionalizing its idea of diaspora philanthropy as a CSR program, which Jaime Augusto describes as "align[ing] profit making with national development goals," institutionalizes diasporic homeland orientations in opposition to radicalized labor and deeper political economic analyses.[64]

Diaspora and Donations: "Easy as 1-2-3"

The (now-defunct) home page of AF-USA described the organization as working to "create opportunities for Filipinos in the U.S. to help the Philippines by facilitating meaningful contributions to social development initiatives."[65] The website also stated that because it partners with more than one hundred NGOs in the Philippines, "AF-USA is able to address the country's greatest needs. We assist Filipinos committed to helping the homeland in supporting projects closest to their hearts."[66] Ideas such as "meaningful contributions" and "the country's greatest needs" are circumscribed by the dual commitment to profit and the market. They limit the nature of the giving relationship, which is disconnected from the economic conditions that structure the country's greatest needs. To this end, AF-USA emphasizes the *ease* with which Filipino Americans can belong to the Filipino diaspora and therefore to the Philippine homeland by donating through its system, an ease that stands in contrast to the fraught associations and accusations of betrayal that often mark the relationship between Filipino Americans and the homeland. For Filipinos in the United States in particular, "leaving the Philippines is tantamount to a betrayal of sorts, a nonfulfillment of an obligation to contribute to the nation."[67] While remittances support one's family, AF-USA offers an opportunity to easily fulfill larger national obligations through donor participation in its program. AF-USA offers the following "Donor Flowchart" to encourage the Filipino American diaspora, written as its Filipino American donor market, strategically emphasizing the simplicity of "making a difference" in the Philippines: "Making a donation to the Philippines can be as easy as 1-2-3! Step 1. Determine where your donation will go. Step 2. Determine how you want to make your donation. Step 3. Enjoy the satisfaction of making a difference in the Philippines."[68] Inequality, social needs, and the creation and maintenance of poverty disappear in this model of giving, but AF-USA offers a sense of homeland belonging through "the satisfaction of making a difference in the Philippines," personalizing and depoliticizing collective problems.

The Ayala Foundation's public materials fail to describe the qualifications necessary for inclusion as one of its partner organizations in the Philippines, except that partner organizations must be a "legitimate" nonprofit organization, implement projects with "direct impact on the country's areas of greatest needs," and be deemed "worthy of public support by donors in the United States."[69] "Legitimate" organization means an organization has been granted donee status by the Philippine Council for NGO Certification, underlying the bureaucratic and corporate nature of the nonprofit industry and its hold on social change.[70] While many of the organizations describe the services they provide to their communities in the Philippines on the AF-USA website, there is no discussion by the Ayala Foundation concerning how areas of need are identified and by whom. Regarding organizations that are "worthy of support by donors in the United States," Tony Acoba describes the process as involving the organization's marketability and not its politics of social change or need:

> The operation involves the U.S. side and the Philippine side. On the Philippine side, over the years we've been recruiting partner NGOs, thinking that that's the only objective—to recruit NGOs. But later we learned that we should also be selective in inviting NGOs to partner with us. . . . We should look at organizations; we should invite organizations to partner with us if they have the capacity to, number one, do a fund-raiser in the U.S. Do they have contacts in the U.S.? Are the projects of this particular organization marketable in the U.S.?[71]

The marketization of Filipino America reduces diaspora giving to a monetary exchange. According to the Ayala Foundation, because Filipino Americans provide the bulk of remittances to the Philippines, they become the "logical market" for partners in social development. While Filipinos in the United States collectively contribute the largest percentage of overseas remittances, constructing Filipino Americans as a market holds implications for how the Ayala Foundation approaches ideas of giving and diaspora. Remittances may signal the possibility of diaspora philanthropy programs to fund-raise in Filipino America, but remittances do not sufficiently fulfill national obligations for Filipino Americans, which the Ayala Foundation connects to making a donation and "the satisfaction of making a difference in the Philippines." Because there is no context for how AF-USA identifies or historicizes the "greatest needs" of the Philippines, it encourages its market to believe that each of the organizations listed contributes to national development or frames need and poverty equally and interchangeably. The projects are not valued for political or economic commitments but for emotional ones ("we assist Filipinos committed to helping the homeland in supporting projects closest to their hearts"), furthering a disconnect among sources of economic problems in the Philippines, diaspora-homeland belonging, and proposed solutions and frameworks for addressing such slippery concepts of inequality and need.

If Filipino Americans are the market, then the various nonprofit organizations listed on the AF-USA website are the commodities, chosen for their marketability to Filipino Americans and their emotional appeal, producing a homeland that extends an individualized fulfillment of an abstract desire to help. The website creates products that are legible for and "saleable" in the Filipino American market.[72] The organizations and projects presented through the "Donate Now" link become interchangeable and equivalent in this process of commodification. In this process, each Philippine-based NGO loses its particularity, obscuring the ways that organizations envision and politicize transformation in the Philippines. The different qualities of specific organizations are transformed into a common unit of measurement—they are all now merely "approved partners" of AF-USA—even if the politics or goals of their organizations may be fundamentally at odds, thus signaling to the diaspora a depoliticized Philippine homeland community and homeland orientation. Organizations are partnered with AF-USA based on their personalized and emotional appeal to the Filipino American market. Its institutionalization of diaspora philanthropy produces a Filipino American subject in relationship to the depoliticized Philippine organizations, promoting a pluralist, multicultural diasporic connection in which the Filipino American subject identifies with the abstract concepts "women," "health," or "education."[73]

The website interface of the donations page fails to differentiate the organizations, which is echoed by the Ayala Foundation's approach to diaspora philanthropy overall. Essentially, it promotes the idea that Filipino Americans should *just give*. While one can argue that philanthropy as it has been institutionalized has been depolit icized so that it either encourages donations to no other transformative end or stabilizes the social system, the Ayala Foundation is significant in its contributions to the discourse on diaspora philanthropy. What matters according to the rhetoric of the Ayala Foundation is that Filipino Americans should simply give and that they should give to the foundation's own list of approved recipients. Mario Deriquito, former director of the Ayala Foundation's Center for Social Development, states:

> Like a murder mystery, Filipino Americans have motive, resources, and opportunity. Incomes are high in a culture where the spirit of philanthropy is high. Most in the U.S. are new immigrants, so there are still strong emotional ties. The Philippine needs to benefit from these ties. Giving is usually to relatives, small infrastructure projects in hometowns, and school

> renovation and scholarship. The potential is in redirecting giving and new donors. It's this potential that AF-USA hopes to unlock. It is the Ayala Foundation USA's goal to redirect current giving practices. Wean them from their localized ways of giving.[74]

It is not my objective here to rank the partner organizations or argue that some are more worthy of support than others. The chapter does not examine specific case studies of the organizations listed as partners of the Ayala Foundation, and I do not claim to grasp the implications of perceived ideological differences among the partner organizations. Terms used by the partner organizations on the Ayala Foundation website to describe their organizational politics such as "family values," "fighting injustice," "the empowerment of women," and "alternative" are emptied of significance and operate as political shorthand.[75] The Ayala Foundation benefits from the perceived ideological range of partner organizations and the illusion that the Ayala Foundation represents the homeland in its entirety and in all of its political ideological leanings. The range of organization choices supports the list of approved partner organizations standing in metonymically for not just the Philippine nation but also the opportunity for homeland belonging.

This foundation, this corporation, and this practice of community obscure other methods of organizing that would contradict how they have guided diasporic giving. The Ayala Foundation has a vested interest to not support organizations that are critical of Ayala, thus controlling the range of organizations available for this version of the Philippine homeland community. For example, AF-USA did not include the IBON Foundation in its list of projects because it had been vocal in the antiprivatization water movement in the Philippines. It tried but was unable to stop Ayala's 1997 purchase of the water distributor Manila Water, Inc., a previously public service. The point is not to encourage Filipino Americans to find the "correct" organization, either to a certain politics or to their own sense of self, to which they can donate. Rather, the focus is on the implications of diaspora giving through an intermediary foundation that actively isolates society from history and political economy, thereby maintaining the global hierarchies that position and construct the Philippines as a premier labor exporter for the world.

Given the status of this corporate foundation, coupled with the ease of making online donations, attention must be paid to the linkages among consumer society and the politics of diaspora giving. As Paul Gilroy describes, "Identity has even been taken into the viscera of postmodern commerce, where the goal of planetary marketing promotes not just the targeting of objects and services to the identities of particular consumers but the idea that any product whatsoever can be suffused with identity. Any commodity is open to being 'branded' in ways that solicit identification and try to orchestrate identity."[76] Even as the internet produces transnational linkages, it enables diaspora formations premised on the individualized support of commodified organizations that are "closest to their hearts." Giving is central to the lives of Filipinos in the United States because it creates the possibility of imagining a different world to which they can belong. As a corporate foundation, the Ayala Foundation erases whatever harms its parent business may cause Filipinos in the Philippines. As a business-oriented mediator that claims to ensure that donations by Filipino Americans "make a difference in the Philippines," the Ayala Foundation creates a gap between Filipino Americans and the realities of poverty in the Philippines, thus emptying their giving of the possibility of its potential for transformation.[77]

Privatization and Poverty: Accessing Water in Manila

The Ayalas, along with the other elite families who control the economy of the Philippines, greatly benefit from the neoliberal, free-market policies adopted by the state that continue to limit social transformation in the Philippines.[78] In 1997, Ayala participated in the water-privatization program for the area surrounding the Metro Manila capital through its company Manila Water, a business transaction that became the largest water-privatization program in the world. The World Bank, the Asian Development Bank, and the Philippine administration all agreed that the deal would ultimately serve the public, an argument that was based on the belief that the private sector can deliver the service more efficiently and with less corruption than the state.

The privatization of water in the Philippines cannot be understood without an understanding of the ascendancy and rule of neoliberal programs through the conditions set by multilateral institutions. The road to water privatization in the Philippines began during Ferdinand Marcos's period of martial law, when the Philippines agreed to move toward the privatization of state-owned assets as a condition for a loan of three hundred million dollars from the World Bank. In efforts to dismantle monopolies that were controlled by Marcos's cronies and support a doomed strategy of debt repayment to international lending agencies, Corazon Aquino issued Presidential Proclamation 50, mandating a "program for the expeditious disposition and privatization of certain government corporations and/or the assets thereof, and creating the committee on privatization and the asset privatization trust." Aquino's successor, Fidel Ramos (president from 1992 to 1998), solidified the process, ushering in a deal with the IMF that specified the privatization of water as one of its conditions for a structural adjustment agreement.[79]

As designed by the International Finance Corporation, water privatization would be implemented through concession contracts wherein private companies would manage existing infrastructure to provide water services and have opportunity to charge users' fees for their services.[80] In exchange for this control, the concessionaires, Manila Water and Maynilad, agreed to a series of provisions intended to protect consumers. The contracts were quickly granted with very little discussion from legislators, underlying the lack of a democratic process, and with a great deal of celebration by Ramos and the multilateral institutions.

The Metropolitan Waterworks and Sewerage System and Ayala promised their consumers that rates would decrease as a result of privatization, but rates in 2006 grew by almost 1,000 percent.[81] In 2004, Manila Water brought in ₱4.164 billion in revenue with ₱1.332 billion in profits, and this rose to ₱8.913 billion in revenue and ₱788 billion—more than $58 million in profits in 2008.[82] The company continues to expand to other areas and provinces in the Philippines and has started providing water-service operations in India and Vietnam.[83]

The privatization of water reflects only one of the ways in which the Ayalas have benefited from neoliberal policies that exacerbate the very poverty that their CSR projects mobilize Filipino Americans to resolve. It clearly demonstrates how visions of social transformation are degraded when attached to fundamental adherence to the ideals of the free market. Critics of this kind of poorly regulated privatization argue that water is an essential component for human life, not a commodity that should be sold by companies that can "refuse to extend their services to anyone within their service area."[84] The issue is whether water is a commodity and can be sold for profit or if it is "for the people,"[85] a social good rather than an economic good or, in international legal discourse, a human right that is outside the market.[86] Manila Water attempts to resolve this tension in the company's 2008 annual report, which displays with apparent seamlessness the relationship between life and profit promoted by neoliberalism and the free market:

> Water has always been essential for life; and as time progresses, its value has significantly escalated. Supplying clean and potable water has been increasingly difficult, primarily because of the depletion of various water resources as well as the growth in the world's population. Thus, water has been perceived as the "new gold rush" and has become an increasingly scarce commodity. Manila Water sees this situation as an opportunity to grow.[87]

As it does for some of its other companies, Ayala looks for these opportunities to grow in profits and capital by creating products that can be sold to the very poor, who for this case in the Philippines, are referred to as the "emerging market."

Manila Water is in business and the Ayala Foundation is in operation because they claim that they can do their work more efficiently than the state. Each time Ayala or the Ayala Foundation touts its efficiency, it makes an implicit reference to a faith in the ability of the market to solve society's problems and the endemic corruption of the Philippine state. Structural adjustment of the 1980s and 1990s and neoliberal policies of privatization, deregulation, and trade liberalization are based on the same argument: growth and development are by-products of efficiency, and the market achieves efficiency through market-oriented policy.[88] Neoliberalism and free-market policies, as marketed by its proponents, are fantasies of social change: economic growth, produced through a market that operates with minimal interference from the state, produces peace and prosperity. As major corporations give back to the communities through their large-scale corporate social-development programs, it becomes more difficult to intervene in global capitalism itself. These are the terms offered by their dream for Filipinos and for Filipino American diaspora philanthropy.

Filipinos cite corruption as the number-one obstacle to development in the Philippines; it is the commonsense explanation for why the Philippines fell behind so many of its regional neighbors. This discourse deems corrupt individual public officials as the source of widespread inequality and conditions of poverty and minimizes larger political economic critique. Economist and vocal critic of corporate-driven globalization Walden Bello argues that this common sense serves to maintain the neoliberal policies that support the ruling power elite.[89] As Bello states, "While corruption definitely needs to be condemned, it is not the reason behind the country's stagnation. A more adequate explanation lies in the state being subjugated by a succession of ruling elite factions to serve narrow interests instead of the larger goals of sustainable development and social justice."[90] Ruling elites incorporate these narrow interests into their CSR programs, extensions of their business philosophies, which, in the case of Ayala and its foundations, circumscribe their institutionalization of diaspora philanthropy that compels identification with the homeland.

While Bello's argument hinges on the inabilities of a weak state controlled by alternating factions of the business/political elite, the Ayalas are no longer as politically active as they once were and have taken a back seat to most of the Philippine oligarchic clans. This was not always the case; Jaime Zobel de Ayala, chairman emeritus of Ayala and chairman of the board and Executive Committee of the Ayala Foundation, was appointed Philippine ambassador to the Court of St. James's in the United Kingdom and the Scandinavian countries from 1970 to 1975. The Ayalas publicly supported Corazon Aquino's run for presidency against Marcos in the 1986 snap election, ushering in what economist Kenji Koike calls the "honey moon period between the Aquino government and the Ayala family" that set up the family corporation to be the extensive conglomerate that it is today.[91] The Ayalas also vigorously lobbied for the resignation of

Joseph Estrada, the self-proclaimed president of the poor who voted for him en masse. States Jaime Augusto:

> As a group, we try to keep business and politics separate, which is not particularly easy to do in a country like the Philippines. But while we try to help out behind the scenes in pushing for reform, there were two notable occasions when we expressed our concerns quite vocally. The first was in 1986, when the original People's Power movement succeeded in deposing then-President Marcos, and the second was during the impeachment proceedings against then-President Estrada, early last year. In both instances, we felt strongly that the public trust had been violated to such an extent that the continuation of these men in power would almost certainly have plunged our country into economic and social chaos.[92]

The Ayalas purportedly act only in the name of protecting the public good, legitimizing their ability to lead what they claim are transparent efforts toward national development. Some mainstream news outlets were not convinced. According to *Asiaweek* reporters in regard to the family's vocal protest against Estrada, "Jaime Augusto expressed concern that the populist president might stir up a class war to rally his supporters, pitting rich against poor. That could lead to public disturbances in tony Makati, an exclusive residential and business district that Ayala Corp. developed."[93]

Elite factions of the political and economic structure of the Philippines align with each other and fight to maintain power to maximize potential economic gain. Writes Walden Bello, "It became fashionable in line with the reigning neoliberal ideology to speak about the state suffocating the creativity of the market, but the fundamental reality that linked the Marcos period, the Cory Aquino period, and the post-Cory Aquino period was *the existence of an unchanging class structure, in which asset and income distribution was one of the worst in the developing world*."[94] Bello specifically includes the Ayalas as vital players among the Philippine ruling elite, a bold move given the virtually "untarnished" reputation to which the Ayalas are accustomed.[95] While Jaime Zobel de Ayala and his two sons, Jaime Augusto and Fernando, are consistent and dedicated advocates of "corporate citizenship," their corporate dealings dictate the reach of their social-responsibility programs, including those of AF-USA.

Empirically, Bello argues that there are numerous other countries that suffer from as much as or even more widespread political corruption than the Philippines but have greatly surpassed the Philippines in reducing poverty.[96] Politicians, multilateral institutions, and reporting agencies hold, almost universally, corruption as the source of poverty in the Philippines. As argued by Bello, corruption discourse serves the interests of the free market and neoliberal enterprise: "The discourse is also very useful for those who gain from the policy agenda of neoliberalism, the theoretical foundation of which will crumble without the threat of corruption."[97] It is "one of the lynchpins that hold the neoliberal discourse together."[98] The discourse of corruption allows the ruling elites to blame the extensive poverty of the Philippines on the government and to present themselves as the solution through their purported adherence to self-imposed corporate codes. As argued by David Harvey, "There exists a curious penchant to pursue 'corruption' as if it is easily distinguishable from the normal practices of influence-peddling and making money in the marketplace."[99] Anticorruption initiatives guide the U.S.-backed World Bank's involvement in the Philippines and the UN's dealings with the Philippines, and it affects the corporate and foundational rhetoric of the Ayalas. Ayala's links to anticorruption reform programs are numerous, as is its record for commodifying natural resources and approaches to social change.[100]

Conclusion

The Philippine-based Ayala Foundation created AF-USA, a California-based nonprofit organization, to assure potential Filipino American donors that their donations would go to legitimate, Ayala Foundation–approved organizations in the Philippines. I acknowledge the dedication of scores of people that facilitate their programs and recognize the relative poverty of the Philippines in relation to that of the United States and the desire of Filipinos in the United States to maintain an orientation to the Philippines by giving back. This does not, however, remove the imperative to trace the institutionalization of diaspora philanthropy that masks the structures that perpetuate poverty in the Philippines. Through the presentation and reiteration of ahistorical, apolitical fictions of homeland and belonging, the complexity and implications of diaspora giving are lost.

Neoliberal market logics work to undermine the possibilities of giving and diaspora as critical spaces with the potential for coalition and the fostering of an anti-imperialist politics. Ayala supports its global corporate citizenship programs and the Ayala Foundation while simultaneously expanding the neoliberal project through the privatization of water and the Philippines' exploited position in the global capitalist economy. The Ayala Foundation partners with a range of NGOs in the Philippines, incorporating the differences among the organizations through their commodification and concealing the implications of the organizations' differences in terms of frameworks of need and social transformation. Corporations deal with the contradictions of public goods, public infrastructure, and public interests in the service of private profit through their CSR programs. Rooted within this understanding is a logic grounded in a system that supports the expansion of capital, the containment of radical or revolutionary politics, the racialization and gendering of the Philippine labor force, and the belief that profit-driven projects will solve society's ills.

Ayala and its foundations offer solutions and programs for problems in the Philippines, but their solutions and programs mask the historical context and economic conditions of the problems as well as other practices of giving by Filipinos in America. The Ayala Foundation constructs the Philippine nation in opposition to radical platforms, extending its desire for a diaspora and homeland that would erase such struggles, concealing the transformative possibilities of a diaspora-giving imagination that could maintain a critique of the ruling elites and the stratified distribution of land that maintains inequality in the Philippines.

4

Philippine Environments and Critical Ecologies of Diaspora Giving

Some of the most urgent and organized calls for diaspora giving within Filipino America are made in the wake of natural disasters in the Philippines. These calls animate public conversations within Filipino American diaspora about what it means to give responsibly in a way that is particular to the cultural work of "nature" and "the environment." Deciding which organizations to sponsor as a Filipino American enters public discourse during, and after, these moments of catastrophic geological destruction. Filipino Americans must weigh factors such as a charity's capacity to deliver donations directly to the neediest individuals, an organization's level of overhead, and the urgency of both preventive and service-providing programs in sites of devastation. Filipino Americans recently engaged in these kinds of discussions in the aftermath of Typhoon Haiyan (named Yolanda in the Philippines) that devastated Leyte in the Visayas region in 2013.[1]

These public conversations extend more readily when recipients of aid are seen as victims, suffering from causes beyond their control. These conversations about giving responsibly are much quieter—if not absent—in regard to ameliorating poverty and its effects, for many of the reasons that are the concerns of *Giving Back*. This plays out in how recipients of aid are written in the dominant discourse as at least partially responsible for their own impoverishment. As the previous chapter discusses, individualized, market-oriented solutions in Filipino American diaspora are dominant. And the desire to do good, which Chapter 1 addresses, can become the goal of giving in and of itself. The resulting diasporic practice is depoliticized: anything you do to give back as a Filipino American is a benefit for the Philippines because its people are so poor. Such constructions of diaspora giving demonstrate how certain narratives of giving back fetishize benevolence, separating the space of homeland from transnational historical and economic conditions that bind the Philippines to the United States and to the structural reproduction of poverty.

This chapter discusses this tendency to isolate the Philippine environment from the conditions of its production. To speak of the vulnerability of the Philippines to natural disaster without narrating its production as third-world space is to naturalize its helplessness. This vulnerability is the flip side of the image of the Philippines as an island paradise, but the two imaginings exist in parallel.[2] Diaspora giving, for example, can call attention to the environment and preservation of the beauty of the homeland, to the resuscitation of precolonial or indigenous vegetation, and to justice for communities that bear the environmental costs of industrial growth. All of these draw on and contribute to their own sets of knowledge regarding the Philippine homeland environment. Bringing a critical diaspora giving analysis to the Philippine environment unsettles romanticized sentiments of the Philippine island wonderland. Addressing critical environmental politics in his book on forest politics in British Columbia, radical geographer Bruce Braun explains that most accounts of forest politics assume the forest to hold an "unproblematic identity," thus producing solutions to complex social conflicts over the forest in terms of either preservation or restoration. Braun instead "asks how something called the 'forest' is made visible, how it *enters history* as an object of economic and political calculation, and a site of emotional and libidinal investment."[3] For Filipino Americans, the emotional and material investments in the environmental homeland are directed at a space that is always already economic and political in nature; this position confronts the ideological investments of representations that insist on its eternal beauty.

The focus on the environment is not incidental to the larger consideration of diaspora giving. Ecological projects are social projects that link ideas of difference, gender, race, and nation and thus are inseparable from power relations.[4] While projects and politics dealing with the environment conjure the natural space or landscape of the Philippine homeland more readily than other development schemes or social movements, it is vital to recognize the construction of the environment in its specific iterations. I am concerned with the processes by which diaspora giving can challenge the hierarchies of power at the intersection of neocolonialism, global capitalism, and developmentalism. One site where these hierarchies become apparent is in mobilization of the Philippine environment.

This chapter examines the iconography of the Philippine environment as an island paradise displayed in travel guides and the marketing of the Philippines' cultural-environmental particularity, tracing the reverberations of the Philippines as a timeless place of beauty in giving back. The chapter turns to an examination of a particular transnational Filipino American organization, FACES, a U.S.-based environmental-justice organization originally founded to bring attention to, and reparations for, the environmental devastation wrought by former U.S. military bases in the Philippines. Originally, the goals of FACES were largely technical and clear-cut: it would pressure the U.S. military to take economic and legal responsibility for the toxic materials abandoned at the site of its former military bases via both a public awareness campaign and litigation against the U.S. government. The organization lost its court cases and appeals, and the Philippine environment was determined to be outside the U.S. military's legal responsibility. After these litigious failures, however, its leaders began the intellectual labor necessary for developing a curriculum for Filipino Americans on neocolonial economic and social structures as a political requisite for diasporic solidarity and coalition work in the Philippines. In so doing, it rearticulated a disorienting Filipino American diaspora-giving politics.

This chapter traces how FACES reorients dominant diaspora-giving practices by connecting environmental issues in the Philippines to environmental issues in the United States and elsewhere. Its framework for social transformation amounts to an expansive mobilization of Filipino American diasporic subjectivity in which responsibility as a Filipino American leads to solidarity with Filipinos in the Philippines through issues that stem from the Philippines' subordinate position in the global order. This subsequently opens a space for action in solidarity with non-Philippine spaces and non-Filipino peoples who are exploited and made vulnerable by global capitalism. Refracted through the efforts of people who act as self-identified Filipino Americans, a diasporic politics can critically assess, if not dislodge, dominant giving relationships.

The Philippine Environment as Paradise

The Philippines is not at the top of the list of premier destinations for Western and wealthy adventurers, a fact of eternal concern for the country's Department of Tourism and travel agencies. The relatively low rates of tourism, especially when compared to those of other Southeast Asian countries, are often seen as a result of the country's weak infrastructure, unfavorable press regarding reports of terrorism on the southern island of Mindanao, and the current president's support of extrajudicial killings, which are committed in the name of drug control. The following is a typical travel-guide description of what tourists can expect to find in the Philippines:

> All her neighbours have magical tourist appeal, but the Philippines, even though the sea is just as blue and clear and the myriad coral islands just as alluring, seems to have missed the boat when it comes to fully marketing its attractions. Bad press in recent years, after some high-profile terrorism and kidnapping incidents, ha[s] not helped matters. The country has also laboured under a turbulent political reputation and is still overcoming the effects of martial law. Its poor infrastructure, dilapidated roads and unsafe ferries, have also all played a role in deterring potential travellers and the country has been overlooked as an eco-tourist destination because of local disregard for its natural resources (such as fishermen dynamiting coral reefs). . . . The good news is that Filipinos themselves are warm and welcoming—as underscored in the country's tagline—"where Asia wears a smile."[5]

This travel guide represents the Philippines as on the verge of being a premier travel destination—that it *could* be a staple of ecotourists' dreams for its requisite blue seas, coral reefs, and beaches if not for the negative press. Reported threats of Islamic terrorism and political upheaval scare away would-be tourists and their tourist dollars, and the environment exists as far as it is made available to meet consumer tourist demand for paradise-like conditions, guiding the kinds of interventions that can be made on its behalf. Destruction or abuse of the environment is mourned not for its effects on the health, quality of life, and livelihoods of Filipinos but for its arrest of an ecotourism industry, resulting in the environmental elaboration of consumerism and commodification.[6] Prioritizing consumption within environmental affairs circumscribes the possibilities of environmentalism and produces an agent of the environment as either a person outside the Philippines (a privileged visitor), a privileged Filipino returnee, or a member of the country's elite.

Access to livelihoods and widespread poverty is of concern in this vision of the environment only insofar as it impedes the development of an ecotourism industry. Those Filipinos who bear the weight of underdevelopment are taken out of environmental concerns, their labor and bodies serving the needs of Western consumer demands and made into part of the landscape itself. Taking care of others, this Filipino subject has resonance with the "Great Filipino Worker," the Philippines' most prized export to countries abroad.[7] The refrain from travel agencies—Filipino and non-Filipino alike—generally celebrates the people of the Philippines and their positive attitudes, making the long flight to the islands worth the price of the airfare. The landscape as paradise envelops the local Filipinos, who are represented as a capital investment or as a resource to promote the beauty of the environment and worthiness of ecotourist dollars, diverting attention from plays of power and privilege that enable a tourist's entitlement. While there may be Islamic terrorists and political uprisings, the warmth, hospitality, and smiles of the Filipinos work to mitigate the inconveniences a tourist might encounter because of the conditions of poverty and infrastructural deterioration.

Thus, the Philippines' own identity as the place "where Asia wears a smile" performs ideological work beyond the masking of widespread poverty and labor exploitation. The smiles do the ideological work of containing political protest and dissent, presenting the people as essentially content and harmless, and advocating a toothless environmentalism that is defined against movements for social change. This environmental imagery can be directly linked to the inception and sexualization of the country's tourism industry that developed during the martial-law era of Ferdinand Marcos. As stated by Cynthia Enloe in her influential *Bananas, Beaches, and Bases*, "Marcos and his advisors, with encouragement from foreign banks and technical consultants, had viewed tourism as a primary building block of development. The regime had used the reputed beauty and generosity of Filipino women as 'natural resources' to compete in the international tourism market."[8] The dominant sexualization and investment in the Filipina who is located in proximity to red-light districts designed to service the U.S. military can be found in the way that Jesse "The Body" Ventura, former governor of Minnesota, sings the country's praises:

> I loved the Philippines. I was stationed at Subic, and I loved going into Olongapo. It was more like the Wild West than any other place on earth. In Olongapo, there's a one-mile stretch of road that has 350 bars and 10,000 girls on it every night. . . . To the kid I was then, it was paradise. . . . When a girl went with you in Olongapo, there was no question about what you were going to do.[9]

Sex tourism in the Philippines is part and parcel of the environment as island paradise, and the beauty of the Philippine paradise corresponds to the availability and sexualization of Filipinas. Ventura participates in a discourse that constructs the Philippines as paradise, requiring a "suspension of a critique of the neocolonial Philippine economy [that] ensures and distinguishes the privileged positions these men occupy in Philippine society."[10]

In its essentialism, the environment exists outside politics, its timeless beauty unmarred by violent struggles over resources, land use, tenant farming, and ownership. The representation of nature's separation from politics and culture enables lamentations of the deterioration and general degradation of the country only insofar as it depreciates the value of its beauty but not of its paradise essence, which is held far from the poverty that taints it. Calling attention to the environment's construction disrupts this essentialist representation and brings to the surface the ideological work of particular iterations of nature and the environment by "buttressing certain beliefs, warranting actions, justifying forms of society, and naturalizing hierarchical social relations."[11]

The tendency to narrate the environmental space of the Philippines through its beauty and the simultaneous declaration and dismissal of the conditions of life for many Filipinos extends beyond marketing. Filipino Americans also participate in the circulation of this discourse. Filipino American studies sociologist Rick Bonus observes a tendency among first-generation Filipinos in the United States to describe the Philippine homeland as "pure, natural, and paradise-like."[12] "That's how we want to remember the Philippines," describes one Filipino American.[13] Bonus considers their reaction an expression of the difficulties of immigrant life, a coping mechanism in the face of racism or unexpected circumstances in the United States. This description of a Philippine paradise holds significant reverberations for Filipino American diaspora giving. The idealization of the space of the Philippines as paradise by Filipino Americans, even though produced as a coping mechanism stemming from the difficulties of the racialized ethnic immigrant experience, draws on narratives or fictions of the beauty and innocence of the homeland and separates the conditions of their racialization from their diaspora-giving politics.

Consider the following description of Filipino American diaspora giving from my interview with Angelo Alaan, an active leader in the Filipino American community and a current and past president and board member of multiple Filipino American associations and organizations, most of which engage in programs of giving back:

> As I said, we do a lot of charitable giving to the Philippines. It shows the good heart of Filipinos. Filipinos in the U.S. can help Filipinos in the Philippines in many ways. One is keeping our pride and honor in being Filipino Americans, because if they hear us saying we're proud to be a Filipino or I'm proud that I originated from the Philippines—they hear that in the Philippines, especially those hard-up people—then morale goes up, and they become proud of themselves. They have problems in the Philippines, but we should emphasize more the good

> things in the Philippines, like what we do find good, especially Filipino characteristics. We have a great Filipino character, and we are beautiful as a people. We are a beautiful and hospitality-minded people, and the Philippines is very beautiful. I always mention that to my friends. We have a beautiful country, the Philippines, and lots of great natural resources. So what I'm saying is talk positively about the Philippines and the people because that's us, actually.[14]

Beginning his response about charitable giving in the Philippines, Alaan quickly moves to a commentary about national pride in being Filipino. The Philippine environment, he claims, is powerful enough to regenerate stunted pride in being Filipino, dissolving boundaries between the beauty of the land, the beauty of Filipino people, and his own rationale for giving back from diaspora.

Recognizing the beautiful homeland of the Philippines becomes the extent of giving in itself. In his gesture to the difficulty of "keeping our pride and honor in being Filipino Americans" and from the Philippines ("because that's us, actually"), Alaan alludes to the degradation of Filipinos in the popular imagination, the well-established image of exploitable laborers, efficient yet cheap and valued for their mobility. He confronts his racialization with a commitment to giving, but, he argues, the greatest charity would be for Filipino Americans to have pride in themselves, encouraging even the most impoverished in the Philippines toward psychic and, ostensibly, material betterment. Despite the problems within the Philippines, Filipinos must, above all, be recognized for their hospitality and the country exoticized for its beauty. Romanticizing the homeland by Filipino Americans in this narration of the Philippines as a paradise overlaps with marketing the Philippine environment to elite consumers. Each separates the environment or the homeland, respectively, from relations of power and elides the material realities that set off descriptions and memories of beauty and fantasy from degradation, poverty, and political unrest.

To romanticize the Philippine environment is to isolate its utility and history from forces of neocolonialism, global capitalism, and developmentalism. A striking example of the imagery of the romanticized Philippine environment can be located in another leading travel guide, from the Lonely Planet Company, which again demonstrates the ubiquity and currency of the discourse:

> The Philippines is defined by its emerald rice fields, teeming megacities, graffiti-splashed jeepneys, smouldering volcanoes, bug-eyed tarsiers, fuzzy water buffalo and smiling, happy-go-lucky people. . . . More adventurous travellers can pitch a tent on a deserted stretch of coastline in Palawan and play solo *Survivor* for a few days. . . . Vestiges of the Spanish era include exuberant town fiestas (festivals) and centuries-old stone churches. Malls, fast-food chains and widespread spoken English betray the influence of Spain's colonial successor, the Americans. Yet, despite these outside influences, the country remains its own unique entity. The people are, simply, Filipinos—and proud of it. Welcoming, warm and relentlessly upbeat, it is they who captivate and ultimately ensnare visitors.[15]

These excerpts represent the Philippines, like other countries in the Global South, as a paradise, catering to those both calm and wild, while poverty is brightened by the ebullience of the native population. The landscape of the Philippines is first and foremost a place of beauty and wonder, a characterization that isolates nature in the Philippines from social and cultural forces that make the space of the Philippines available to neocolonial imagery. Lonely Planet describes a fantasy that rewrites the legacy of colonization into a cultural tapestry, where past colonization is celebrated for increasing the islands' value as a tourist destination, itself made possible by neocolonial discourse. Such a description connects the contemporary Philippines as a landscape for tourists as the final frontier during U.S. expansion into the Pacific, a place for masculine renewal when rugged Americans mourned the taming of its western boundary by the late 1800s.[16] In both iterations, the Philippine landscape is a playground for a Western interloper, colonizer, or tourist, an environment that erases its peoples, its wars, and its history, facilitating environmentalisms that parallel those elisions. Romanticizing colonial relationships, today's environmental tourist industry updates the mandate of colonizers from the century past, containing militancy and protest in a depoliticized relationship resonant of the benevolent taming of the

Filipino insurrection in the Philippine-American War. The environment of the Philippines, as widely represented, naturalizes hierarchal social relations, supporting an environmentalism that silences the neocolonial other by fusing the Filipino with the environment.

Environmental-justice politics gained popularity in part for its pressing critique of mainstream environmentalism's historical inattention to the marginalization of people of color and of working people in policy debates and environmental decision-making.[17] Whereas many observers critique mainstream environmentalism for its primary investments in conservation and preservation projects, environmental-justice movement politics also insists on emphasizing that racialized and indigenous populations, working and poor communities, and women have had to carry the burden of progress, living and laboring near waste facilities in a polluted environment. The environmental-justice movement relates these issues to larger struggles for participatory democracy and access to health care, education, safe housing, nontoxic food, and social services.

FACES is an environmental-justice organization that intercedes in dominant homeland orientations that maintain a natural and timeless connection between Filipinos in America and the Philippine homeland. Raising important questions about responsibility, accountability, solidarity, and the terms of giving to the Philippines, the organization situates the Philippine environment within its historical, social, and political economic production. Reaching these commitments, however, was a process that began with failure for the organization.

At its inception in 2000, FACES was an advocacy organization and operated under a slightly different name, one that carries significant implications for its environmental and diasporic politics. FACES stood for Filipino/American Coalition for Environmental "Solutions," the last word reflecting the organization's goal of forcing the U.S. military to take economic and legal responsibility for the management of its hazardous waste left in the Philippines. The organization lost its legal cases and appeals in 2003 and 2005, respectively, and its members were forced to reevaluate the organization's overall mission, including its singular orientation to Philippine communities affected by environmental injustice. Since 2005, the "S" in FACES has stood for "Solidarity." It now commits itself to fostering unity with communities who are fighting environmental injustice. While this Filipino American organization involves itself with issues that are considered most urgent by its partner organizations and communities within the Philippines, the injustices suffered by its partner communities exceed territorial mappings because of the global reach of multinational corporations and the U.S. military. In developing programs and actions in tandem with partners both in and outside the Philippines, in creating an environmental-justice curriculum through the history of U.S.-Philippine neocolonial relations, and in leading Philippine homeland return trips for young Filipino Americans to learn about and experience the hard work of solidarity building with communities in the Philippines, FACES produces a *disorienting* politics of diaspora giving.

FACE*Solutions*, Environmental Responsibility, and the Territoriality of the Philippines

FACE*Solutions* (the designation I use to refer to the organization prior to its change to FACE*Solidarity* in 2005) was originally conceived in 2000 as a Filipino American advocacy group that hoped to gain the attention of the U.S. Congress for the massive destruction wrought in the Philippines by the U.S. military and to support legal action against the U.S. Department of Defense to acknowledge and take responsibility for the extent of its damage. The former U.S. military bases in the Philippines, like all military bases, are not isolated islands, contained by chain-link fences and signs regulating who belongs and who is forbidden in the demarcated zones. The hazardous waste abandoned on the sites of the former military bases directly and fatally affected the lives, health, and livelihoods of the peoples of Zambales and Pampanga provinces in the Philippines.

According to a 1992 U.S. General Accounting Office report, the naval facility lacked a complete sewage and treatment system and discharged untreated sewage and wastewater directly into Subic Bay. Naval repair facilities dumped lead and other heavy metals directly in the water or buried the metals in landfill. Power plants emitted untreated pollutants into the air, firefighting facilities with no drainage systems left fuel and chemicals to seep directly into the soil and water table, and waste-filled underground storage tanks lacking leak-detection equipment were left to slowly deteriorate.

None of these waste-management tactics comply with U.S. standards and would not be allowed on U.S. soil. The U.S. military never denied the disastrous state of the land and water, but it refuted its responsibility to the Philippine communities and environment. The report from the U.S. General Accounting Office stated:

> Although the Air Force and the Navy have identified significant environmental damage at both Clark Air Base and the Subic Bay Navy Facility, the current basing agreement does not impose any well-defined environmental responsibility on the United States for environmental cleanup and restoration. However, according to Air Force and Navy officials, if the United States unilaterally decided to clean up these bases in accordance with U.S. standards, the costs for environmental cleanup and restoration could approach Superfund proportions.[18]

Superfund refers to the Comprehensive, Environmental Response, Compensation and Liability Act (CERCLA) of 1980, used interchangeably with the Superfund mentioned in the 1992 report. The U.S. Congress enacted CERCLA on the heels of the Love Canal disaster of the 1970s in the hopes of creating a new direction and reputation for environmental responsibility for the U.S. government. CERCLA compels responsible parties to attend to abandoned hazardous-waste sites and maintains a trust fund (the Superfund) for the cleanup of hazardous waste when responsible parties cannot be legally established.[19] As the court decision regarding the former military bases in the Philippines held, parties are responsible only for abandoned hazardous-waste sites when those waste sites are on U.S. soil. After the bases were returned to the Philippines, the U.S. Department of Defense no longer bore legal responsibility to the environment or the peoples in the surrounding areas.

The fight to hold the U.S. government legally responsible for the hazardous-waste cleanup was, of course, an uphill battle from the onset. According to environmental legal scholar Margot Laporte, after an overseas military base "is returned to the host nation, the [U.S. Department of Defense] may not fund any remediation beyond that required by a binding international agreement or under an approved remediation. . . . Because most international agreements do not include specific provisions regarding environmental remediation, the United States is generally under no obligation to comply if the host nation requests remediation."[20] In 2003, FACE*Solutions* brought a precedent-setting legal suit against the U.S. government, seeking the international enforcement of the CERCLA environmental legislation. The case, filed by FACES; ARC Ecology, a California-based environmental-justice organization; and thirty-six Philippine residents in the Subic and Clark vicinities who linked their cancer, blood disease, and children's birth defects to the toxicity in their soil and water, was dismissed.

The court ruled that CERCLA was not intended to apply overseas.[21] The U.S. Division of Environmental and Natural Resources of the Justice Department and its assistant attorney general, Thomas L. Sansonetti, were jubilant over the success in establishing the extraterritoriality of the former military bases. In the division's 2004 "Summary of Litigation Accomplishments," Sansonetti writes, "I am pleased to present the Environment and Natural Resources Division's ('ENRD') Accomplishments Report for Fiscal Year 2004. The Division continues to work tirelessly to enforce and defend America's environmental laws, ensuring the air we breathe is clean, the water we drink pure, and the majestic American landscape preserved for generations to come. This year produced even more record-breaking accomplishments of which all Americans can be proud."[22] The portion of the report addressing the dismissal of *ARC Ecology v. Air Force and Navy* appears under the subheading "Protecting the Public Fisc," an abhorrent turn in the use of protection of federal budgets and dismissal of environmental care: "A significant portion of the Division's practice includes resolving liability of federal agencies in connection with cleanup of contaminated facilities under CERCLA. This year ENRD successfully defended numerous claims of federal Superfund liability, saving the government hundreds of millions of dollars."[23] Concerning the U.S. budget for environmental calamity, the Philippines thus deserves no such protection. The clean air, pure water, and majestic landscapes protected by the Division of Environmental and

Natural Resources are directly maintained through the negation of its responsibility for the Philippine environment.

On appeal in 2005, the U.S. Court of Appeals for the Ninth Circuit ruled against the plaintiffs, stating that the lawyers failed to prove their legal case. The Ninth Circuit judge ruled that CERCLA "cannot be applied extraterritorially to regulate environmental harm overseas" because "the statute overcomes the presumption against extraterritoriality."[24] While Congress has the power to legislate activities overseas for U.S. citizens and entities, statutes that do not expressly state this must overcome what the courts call a "strong presumption against extraterritoriality."[25] The presumption of the courts against extraterritoriality underlines the court's hesitation to "authorize the application of laws that may conflict with laws of another sovereign state," so the courts presume that congressional legislation expresses a domestic territorial focus.[26] The decision terminated the attempt by FACE*Solutions* to secure financial redress from the United States.

Sociologist Valerie Kuletz documents a "geography of sacrifice" in which the government and industry identify expendable spaces for pursuits known to destroy the environment, such as those for weapons testing, nuclear development, and uranium mining. Kuletz writes of lands destroyed by nuclear testing: "Fifty years of the unbridled pursuit of nuclear power have obscured a geography of sacrifice that, when mapped, shows how racism, militarism, and economic imperialism have combined to marginalize a people and a land that many within government and industry, consciously or not, regard as expendable."[27] The U.S. government thus produces the Philippines as a "highly militarized sacrificial landscape" and not a space worth protecting.[28]

FACE*Solutions* worked to raise Filipino America's awareness of the U.S. military's treatment of the Philippine environment and surrounding communities as expendable, and the government's response raises several important issues that point to the limitations of a diasporic politics based primarily on legal procedures. In terms of legal redress, the environment—and those most directly related to its contamination—can be protected only as far as U.S. governing bodies create, interpret, and enforce their own environmental laws. The rhapsodic tone of these descriptions demonstrates that "protection" relates not merely to the environment—American or overseas—but also to U.S. coffers tied to the legal victory of the Environment and Natural Resources Division and the U.S. Department of Defense. The U.S. and Philippine governments failed the communities surrounding the former military bases in the Philippines at the levels of military oversight, legislative vision, and judicial interpretation of existing laws. Putting organizational faith in the U.S. legislative and judicial system to hold the U.S. military responsible for the hazardous waste limited the scope of FACE*Solutions* for imagining its orientation to the Philippine environment because the extent of its social critique was contained within the realm of legalities. Speaking more broadly of the environmental-justice movement or of the larger effects of movement organizations' focus on legal justice, political scientist Stephen Sandweiss asserts the compromises made when the environmental-justice movement is singularly focused on legal discourse and policy debate:

> There is a danger to this remedial action to the extent that legal strategies shift movement struggles out of the control of local activists and into the hands of lawyers and national legal organizations. As a result, laws and litigation are seen as the solution to the problem of environmental injustices, as opposed to community empowerment. Instead of being viewed as a means of achieving fundamental systemic change, "environmental justice" becomes redefined and transformed into just another issue for which we need legislation, or a new legal strategy. The entrance of legal groups into the environmental justice field is, in many ways, a detriment to the movement, blunting its ideological edge and diverting its limited resources.[29]

It is very difficult to sustain a transformative diasporic politics that centers on legal recognition because it must abide by the terms set by judicial and legislation systems that favor the U.S. Treasury over the environment of the Philippines, the people of the Philippines, or notions of moral responsibility. But, after its failure, FACE*Solidarity* successfully developed a platform that can more broadly, according to the organization, "encompass the complex and nuanced relationship between the U.S. and the Philippines."[30] FACE*Solutions* failed, but through its failure it began the intellectual labor necessary for building a wider coalition and rearticulating a more critical Filipino American diaspora-giving politics.

FACE*Solidarity* and Diasporic Responsibility

FACE*Solutions* provides an example of the limitations of state-directed and legal-based solutions in diaspora giving, while the transition and reimagination of FACE*Solidarity* illustrate an organization's commitment to the articulation of a Filipino American diasporic identity shaped purposefully with critical attention to the developmentalist and neocolonial hierarchies of race, gender, sexuality, and place. This is not to say that international, diasporic, or transnational organizations should not involve themselves in legal cases or advocate for state responsibility; drawing such a line is not the point of this chapter or this project. Rather, this chapter looks at the path to FACE*Solidarity* as an example of formulating and guiding a diasporic responsibility that attends to the contradictions of contemporary global capital and development and forwards a diasporic identity through an explicit awareness of those contradictions, resulting in new forms of practice.

The work of FACE*Solidarity* disrupts the narrative of the expendability of the Philippine environment. The U.S. military-industrial complex and environmental protection offices of the U.S. federal government, supported by its court system, fought for the Philippine environment to be defined as extraterritorial—a bounded space, distinct from American environments. FACE*Solidarity*'s response to this was an ecological mindedness that countered the legal construction of the environment, which reinforced the neocolonial economic and power imbalance, with a countermapping of Filipino American diasporic responsibility. Also intervening in the popular construction of the environment that entices a tourist Filipino subject eager to reexperience the beauty of the Philippine homeland, FACES fosters diasporic returns made through an environmental-justice politics, in which the unmooring of the Philippines as paradise parallels the troubling of belonging to an originary homeland detached from colonial histories, U.S. militarism, and transnational capitalism.

In the transition from FACE*Solutions* to FACE*Solidarity*, the leadership worked to imagine the enactment of the formula "Filipino-

American identity through social change" and to broaden its vision and mission to "encompass the complex and nuanced relationship between the U.S. and the Philippines."[31] In the documentation of its 2005 biennial national conference, FACES describes the rationale for its name change: "Through the recent FACES assessment process, the need emerged to extend the scope of FACES to capture the broader environmental justice framework. FACES wanted to deepen our notion of 'solidarity' and recognize the reciprocity of our relationship with Philippine partners. This fueled the discussion around the change of 'S' in FACES." At this conference, the organization "decided to broaden FACES' scope of concerns to address transnational issues of environmental justice that impact Filipino communities in both the United States and the Philippines."[32]

The programmatic objectives of the renewed organization include educational programs for Filipino Americans concerning the Philippines and environmental-justice struggles internationally. FACES shapes its diaspora-giving politics through its educational programs, framing the Philippine homeland as a site of critical contestation and connecting Filipino American diasporic identity to global and transnational movements for social and environmental justice. The education curriculum includes the history of colonization in the Philippines, the neocolonial relationship between the United States and the Philippines, the history of peasant and labor resistance in the Philippines, and present-day organizing by communities fighting for environmental justice around the world. The organization demonstrates its commitment to eschew the paternalism and moralism of dominant relationships of giving:

> Through Kamalayan, FACES members will engage in a series of discussions and activities around the meaning of transnational environmental justice and solidarity in relation to our work. We hope that raising our levels of consciousness will ultimately sharpen our work as a US-based environmental justice organization, working with communities and struggles both here in the U.S. and in the Philippines.[33]

FACE*Solidarity* develops a Filipino American consciousness of social justice in the Philippines that is connected to relevant issues and related struggles in other spaces. In its diaspora-giving framework, diasporic subjectivity builds on a component of education; it does not presume to know what is best for the people of the Philippines and strives to understand how they organize themselves and define their own needs and struggles. It is a disorienting diasporic belonging, particularly when contrasted with the popular discourse and nostalgic longings of the Philippines as paradise. Rather than a politics that is steeped in a romanticized nostalgia of the Philippine homeland, which is itself an ironic response to the racialization of Filipino Americans as degraded Americans, the environmental-justice politics of FACES produce a Philippine homeland environment peopled by communities struggling in disparate conditions shaped by U.S. militarism and global capitalism. The construction of the Philippine homeland is connected to the framing of diasporic Filipino identities; here, Filipino Americans are connected to the Philippines not because of the timelessness of being Filipino but because of material and political realities, justice-based organizing and giving, and solidarity.

Diaspora as an analytic forwards critiques of the uneven benefits and violence of globalization and historically situated global hierarchies that divide and order peoples and spaces. Diaspora giving becomes a question of how Filipino American organizations and giving practices can disorient dominant modes and fantasies of homeland return. Most Filipino American organizations and associations with projects for giving in the Philippines do not organize in solidarity with organizations, communities, or social movements in the Philippines. Solidarity, however defined, is not their goal, and it is not my place or intention to impose this as a goal for all instances of social organization. A transformative diasporic politics is formed through an identification as Filipino American mediated by critical associations of responsibility, accountability, and mutuality. An attendant diaspora-giving practice motivates not by the desire to return to a nostalgic homeland but rather a desire to engage with, and participate in, a homeland constituted by a recognition of power relations. Filipinos in the United States desire multiple nostalgic, childhood, preindustrial, and romanticized homeland spaces. However, a radical and transformative diaspora politics intervenes in those identities and spaces, reorienting the terms and relationships among racialized ethnicity, diaspora, nation, and homeland.

I came to know FACE*Solidarity* through interviews with three present and former board members; through analyses of organizational materials, newspaper articles, and materials related to its court case; and through participation with its first annual Face2Face Solidarity Trip in 2005 to the Philippines.[34] After losing its court battle, FACE*Solidarity* designed the Face2Face Solidarity Trip in conjunction with its organizational overhaul. The trip targeted particularly second-generation Filipino Americans, who did not necessarily have a familiarity with the organization but had an interest in environmentalism.

As a "return trip," the Face2Face Solidarity Trip works to redefine homeland and the ways in which multigenerational Filipino Americans find meaning through travel to the Philippines. These trips are generally organized stays in homeland countries for children or grandchildren of emigrants, and they can be sponsored by governments; U.S.-based cultural associations, corporate foundations, and private benefactors; or individuals themselves. The Face2Face Solidarity Trip disrupts the logic of nationalist returns to the homeland that attempt to define an uninterrupted and originary home for second-plus-generation Filipino Americans. Andrea Louie's work on return trips demonstrates that Chinese American youth bring multiple layers of meaning to personalize their experiences to China and emphasizes that these return trips create new transnational understandings of "Chineseness."[35] Through the nuances of her ethnographic work, Louie demonstrates that Chinese Americans complicate nostalgic returns to an originary homeland by rewriting the scripts of official and "authentic" nationalism, creating experiential meanings that merge multiple cultural and historical references.[36] Louie draws attention to new forms of transnational Chineseness based on how participants relate personal experiences, transnational media, and Asian popular culture to homeland, prompting participants to refuse the Chinese government's discourses of ancestral home as a natural space of belonging for overseas Chinese.

Similarly, I argue that the Face2Face Solidarity Trip creates a framework for its participants to rearticulate Filipinoness through their connection to the transnational production of global injustices that prioritize Western capitalist accumulation over Philippine environments. While in general, return trips designate cultural heritage visits to connect ethnic youths to homelands, return trips also figure prominently in giving back, in which the movement and orientation toward the Philippine homeland is enacted by frameworks of giving, by volunteerism and donations, and by an organization's involvement with these projects in the Philippines. Almost all of the Filipino American associations, organizations, and foundations I had contact with and whose leadership I had the opportunity to interview for this book initiated some kind of return trip to present their donations, carry out their medical missions, visit organization-supported projects, or oversee their infrastructural projects on their return trips. These homeland returns often lack a connection to larger institutional and structural critique and attention to one's own involvement in the maintenance of inequality.

The Face2Face Solidarity Trip is FACES's version of a return trip to the Philippines, but as one participant describes, "FACES was good at bringing us questions that we would have never seen if we were just on vacation."[37] Instead of presenting a pristine environment that would then call for its protection, FACES gives meaning to this space through social practices. The trip was designed to "expose participants to the effects of militarism, globalization, and capitalism on local communities and their resources, introduce participants to groups that are fighting for environmental justice in the Philippines, [and] foster a sense of ownership and understanding through a hands-on service learning curriculum."[38] As described by the FACES board of directors, "The main goal of [the Face2Face Solidarity Trip] is to establish meaningful and mutually beneficial relationships and provide concrete bonds of solidarity between Filipino American and Philippine communities."[39] Elsewhere, the chair of the board of directors wrote that the trip intended to "to connect with communities directly impacted by U.S. transgressions in the Philippines."[40] Oriented toward a Philippine homeland and driven by a responsibility as Filipino Americans to fight against U.S. imperialism, the organization provides a context for a critical responsibility in giving practices.

On the 2005 Face2Face Solidarity Trip, the organization led the group of fifteen mostly 1.5- and second-generation Filipino American participants on a ten-day tour of its projects and partnerships in the Philippines. Some partnerships were long-standing, such as the one with Buklod ng Kababihan (Buklod), a labor organization comprising current and former sex workers in the area adjacent to the former naval base. Other partnerships were yet to be fully explored and developed, such as those with organizations in Marilao, Bulacan, where an unregulated battery-recycling plant was dumping waste into the community's water supply.[41] Face2Face Solidarity Trip participants visited toxic hot spots in the Philippines where community members were fighting for recognition that their towns and neighborhoods had been made environmentally uninhabitable. Participants were housed at nonprofit organizations connected with these issues and in the homes of members of those organizations and attended daily lectures by organizers and activists about the history of the strategies and tactics of organizing by the local Filipino groups.

The educational component and principles of FACES were visited on the first day at the Institute for Popular Democracy, a Philippine organization that defines itself "as an agent for democratization in the Philippines and for empowering civil society organizations, popular organizations, and progressive political parties."[42] There, the executive director of the institute set the context for "creating a Filipino and a Filipino American consciousness."[43] He urged the mostly Filipino American group to relate to the Philippines in terms of "justice and social change," which is itself a conceptual remapping of diaspora: "This is something different because colonial experiences are very much a part of who we are as the Philippines." His lecture concerned the political system of the Philippines as having been molded by colonialism and dominated by oligarchy, and he explained his organization's work in coalition building and affecting the economic system in the Philippines, framing the organization's vision against ones that work within the sanctioned political system in which political factions align themselves behind the lesser of the evils of political campaigns. In one of the regrouping sessions, the leaders presented the organizational goals of FACES. They were working to flesh out ideas of reciprocity and solidarity and ways to use the information presented by the Institute for Popular Democracy's executive director to build its Kamalayan Filipino American consciousness-education program.

The focus and missions of the Philippine-based environmental-justice groups and organizations varied. The participants learned of the history of oil corporations Shell and Chevron in Pandacan, Metro Manila, and the corporations' ability to influence policy and maintain oil depots within the boundaries of urban communities. Philippine activists and community members discussed their attempts to organize their neighbors in protest of the alarming levels of benzene and dioxins in their environment. The group spent a day with residents of Marilao, Bulacan, most of whom work at an automotive lead acid battery–recycling plant, Philippine Recyclers, Inc., a subsidiary of Los Angeles–based Ramcar Batteries Inc., which is situated on the banks of the local river.[44] Data and anecdotal evidence reveal high lead content in the water and soil, supporting the suspicion that the recycling plant was contributing to high rates of asthma and cancer-like symptoms in Marilao. The participants heard from a former employee of Philippine Recyclers, whose blood was found to have very high levels of lead and who had recently received death threats from neighbors because of his actions speaking against the company. These threats stemmed from the fear that the company would eventually move to a different location or close down if exposed as a threat to the environment, and his neighbors did not want to lose their jobs. An understanding of the environmentalist dictate to recycle was given new meaning as the participants witnessed the impact of the recycling process on the residents' health and the recycling company's control over the residents' lives.

In Olongapo near the former Subic Naval Base, the participants stayed at the People's Recovery, Empowerment, Development and Assistance Foundation, which assists sexually abused children and child prostitutes in the red-light district that remains in the area even after the formal exit of the military base. They heard a lecture by the foundation's director on the city and provincial government's support of the sex industry in the area, which continues to be frequented by former American servicemen. The participants spent five days interacting with and learning from the member organizations of the local umbrella group, the Metro Subic Network, a campaign-driven coalition that focuses on toxic-waste issues around Subic. One of the organizations, Buklod, is an Olongapo City–based group that organizes current and former prostitutes and advocates for the welfare of Amerasian children in the area. As a member organization of the Metro Subic Network, Buklod held the network's leadership role in 2005, leading the partnership to address the toxic cleanup in the Subic Bay area. The participants of the Face2Face Solidarity Trip were asked to serve as election monitors for the organizational elections; members of Buklod took the participants to the city's red-light district as they canvassed for new members; and members of Buklod and its partner organization, Movement of Amerasians for Solidarity and Social Assistance, joined the FACES group for a night of dining and story exchange.

On the Buklod-led red-light district outing, the spectacle of older, white Americans, many of whom were presumably former military men stationed in the Philippines, drinking with and playing pool with Filipinas in the Olongapo bars did not initially appear to have a purpose for the participants beyond its shock value. The bars were dark, and a few of the customers/clients tried to strike up conversations with members of the group, forcing the Face2Face Solidarity Trip participants to confront their racialized sexualization and their identities as Filipino Americans. Instead of distancing themselves from the figure of the Filipina prostitute who worked this space of "rest and relaxation," one group member agreed to play pool with an older, white American man who had moved to the Philippines because "it is such a beautiful place to be."

It was important for the FACE*Solidarity* organization and for Buklod to demonstrate that the racialized, sexualized, and gendered bodies of the Filipina are integral to narratives of American military masculinity, particularly for this group of Filipino Americans. Buklod significantly affected the participants whom I interviewed; after the trip they were able to link the materiality of environmental injustice, the racialization and sexualization of Filipinas, and U.S. militarism to Filipino American subjectivities. While some of the group had feelings similar to those of participant Miriah Velasco, who "had been overwhelmed with doubt having only been a witness to the socio-economic effects of the U.S. Military's legacy a.k.a. the Red Light District bordering the former Subic Naval Base," many of the participants felt energized by the work that Buklod performed.[45]

Instead of considering themselves neocolonizers who set themselves apart from the rest of the "natives," the participants learned to understand the larger context of the sex trade in the Philippines. FACES confronts the mutual production of giving subjectivities, which undercuts the hierarchal relationship that giving can mediate, a "giving up" of fictions of American exceptionalism in a giving framework that purposefully encounters the entanglements of variously situated Filipinos. During an interview following the trip, Paul Ramos, one of the participants, described his feelings:

> I really liked the vice president from Buklod and her story. She was a prostitute. I was talking to her, and I knew it was an old prostitute group, but I didn't know that all or most of them did that [worked or had worked as prostitutes]. I thought that they had needed educated women to help them build the thing. I didn't know that they started it themselves or that they were [prostitutes]. I was like, okay, tell me about you. "I used to be that [a prostitute]." And I was like, are you sure? . . . Because I didn't see it. And she was the vice president, she's been to New York for all the conferences, and I was like, wow. She had to do it because she's the oldest, and it was her responsibility. Her dad got sick, and so instead of going to high school, she did it. She was there. She was looking for a job, but all the signs were like, "GRO Needed."[46] There were a lot of American military that the businesses catered to, and she fit the role. She had to do it. . . . She's still intelligent; she can talk; she can charm people. She talked about Buklod and then their programs, and then their projects, and then the future.[47]

An interesting omission in Ramos's statement is that he could barely bring himself to use the word "prostitute." Because he was a young man, I presume that Ramos was embarrassed by her job. His incredulity that the vice president had been a prostitute speaks to his preconceived notion of who prostitutes are, what they look like, and how they speak but also to the elisions of U.S. neocolonialism. This exposure trip changed the terms of difference from an essentialist one that saw prostitutes as "other" and inferior to a vision of difference that focused on power and opportunity. His sense of self as a 1.5-generation Filipino American and of the Philippines was altered in a way that could facilitate critical relationships of giving.

Another participant, Jake Allen, a second-generation Filipino American, shows how he became aware of the "hidden truths" of U.S. neocolonialism, an intimation of the ability of FACES to relay the complexity of diaspora giving:

> One pressing issue would be trying to find the balance between living happily and knowing the truth. Like learning the story about the two kids whose mom [who was a member of Buklod] didn't want them to play basketball because she couldn't feed them after. And she would tell them that she wanted them to study more. Like a lot of truths hidden just for people to be happy. A lot of people have to live a kind of lie or just like not telling the truth about certain situations.[48]

Here the hidden truths take on multiple meanings. Allen describes a conversation with a member of Buklod who discouraged her sons from playing outside and pushes them to study so they can succeed in school. In reality, however, as she explained to Allen, she told them to study because of her fear that her children would become hungry from playing basketball and need additional food that she could not afford. Allen's story speaks to the hidden truths of the lack of opportunities for this woman in particular, but there is resonance for its commentary on the hidden truths of neocolonialism in and the economic reality of the Philippines. Allen, like Ramos, was influenced by his experience, as shown in his reaction to Buklod's dedication as an organization: "You hear a lot about color movements or civil rights movements, and you don't hear too much about Filpino American struggles or Philippine struggles. We have our struggles as well. We have people fighting for our struggles."[49] His connection to the struggles in the Philippines, the legacy of U.S. imperialism in the Philippines, and the untold histories of Filipino American organizing are important elements to consider in FACES's politics of diaspora giving.

Through the Face2Face Solidarity Trip, FACES brings members of the Filipino American community to the Philippines. The organizational politics and programs define Filipino American ethnic identity in terms of the potential for a social-justice reorientation toward the Philippines. Because of charity's and philanthropy's history of producing knowledge of self and other that reflects and legitimates the social order, self-critique becomes an intrinsic component of critical diaspora-giving politics. This redefines the possibilities of "home." What starts out as wanting to help those in the Philippines because of one's orientation to the country does not remain a politics of addressing poverty or environmental justice in the Philippines but of addressing poverty and environmental justice in general. Here, giving practices are not about doing good or helping others. Rather, participants were given tools to imagine giving back through subjectivities bound up with those others in the Philippines and other spaces affected by U.S. imperialism, corporate destruction, and environmental injustice.

Conclusion

Critical environmental studies is a useful way to enter these discussions, as ecology emphasizes social and natural connections and relationships. Through a critical ecology one can begin to theorize how Filipino Americans are connected to Filipinos in the Philippines and other Filipinos overseas through dominant and alternative visions of social transformation in the Philippines. Environmentalism is not the only way to get at alternative diasporic subjectivities and identities, but there is something to learn from the way that it emphasizes connections among capitalism, peoples, and spaces.

Like other return trips, FACES targets second-generation Filipino American youth. FACES argues that "in an increasingly global economic, social, and political environment, it is becoming more and more critical to encourage young people to gain awareness and take action on pressing transnational issues."[50] It works to resignify cultural heritage and family genealogy for second-plus-generation youth who do not necessarily carry a deep understanding of Filipino culture. More uniquely than other Philippine return trips for youth, FACES consciously and deliberately works to define the relationship between Filipino and American on its trips, persistently questioning the nature of responsibility Filipino Americans have to the Philippines. It thwarts tendencies to bifurcate identity, fostering a sense of diasporic belonging cognizant of the ways in which the United States and the Philippines are connected. Thus, it sets up the participants to inhabit a sense of homeland disorientation.

All these issues were touched on in a post-trip interview with a Face2Face Solidarity Trip participant, Paul Ramos:

> I really liked [the trip]. I didn't even know it was more political. I thought it would be more environmental, because . . . what got me interested in the first place was the environmental aspect of it, but I guess it comes with it. The political aspect comes with the environmental aspect. But I really like the environmental approach, using that view to see, as a starting point, to look at all these problems that were interconnected. . . . Environmental issues, I've been kind of involved with since high school . . . like toxic waste and recycling. That's what I was really interested in . . . using this environmental way of seeing to be all these other aspects that were political, transnational, governmental—including people. So that's what I like. I really liked it. As a Filipino, I think [it] got more personal because it was [more] environmental [than] if I went to a different, foundation-based tour.[51]

In this telling, the focus on the environment becomes a moment of possibility. Like diaspora, the environment or environmental politics does not necessarily bring together the excesses of global capitalist politics. Ramos compares his experience with FACES to other youth exposure trips that focus on Philippine culture, where culture is defined as being distinct from politics. This lent meaning to Filipino American diasporic identity through his revision of the environment, the Philippine environmental homeland. To theorize diaspora politics outside neoliberal capitalist processes, to think of diaspora as merely the scattering of peoples outside a homeland or as the experiences of migrants, can lead us to a celebration of transnationalism in and of itself, a diasporic landscape that refuses to look at its contradictions and neocolonial histories and presence. FACES fosters a diasporic identity based not on place and cultural heritage, a timelessness rooted in nostalgic longings, but on the geopolitical contingencies of U.S.-Philippine relations. In fact, in an email communication with Ramos about a year after returning from the trip, he wrote, "I am telling you that FACES has not left me hopeless nor jaded [but] rather hopeful and optimistic of the future. . . . I wanna thank each one of you for opening my eyes and allowing me to recognize and be aware of these injustices that are all interconnected, international."[52]

Environmental justice is not merely about the critique of environmental racism or the lack of accountability by transnational capital for its use of poor spaces as a dumping ground for toxic waste. Environmental-justice politics and critical ecologies of diaspora giving allow us to see how society produces vulnerable spaces brought on by the military, industry, tourism, and state governments. Through recognizing this, we can imagine how this toxicity that obstructs potential coalitions and communities as hazardous-waste sites is tied to social divisions and racial, class, gender, and sexual hierarchies. Environmental-justice politics shows how giving practices can work to counter the hegemonic imposition of these divisions and hierarchies from diaspora. FACES rewrites the travel-guide representation of the environment and the tourists' relationship to the beauty of the Philippines and its people. Vigilant giving practices can challenge modernity's philanthropic relationships in which a knowing subject bestows gifts onto needy recipients. Filipino Americans create new accounts of giving, of social change, and of diaspora belonging when they work to challenge the dominant social relationships of giving.

Epilogue

Diasporic Love

This book uses the lens of Filipino American diaspora giving to examine the economies, conditions, and consequences of mobility and diasporic return. The "love of the motherland" from diasporic discourse and the "love of humankind" from the etymological root of philanthropy coalesce in diaspora giving. There is, perhaps, an expectation that this multidimensional love would guide those who want to help toward an evolved ethos of diasporic belonging. However, love for the homeland and a love of humankind are ultimately ineffable methods of belonging. Love and desire (to help, to return, to engage) serve as expressed motivation for diasporic homeland projects, and affective economies of migration and return are, in certain ways, an understood precondition for diasporic return. It is this sense of unquestioned love that requires attention be paid to how complex expressions of loyalty, intimacy, and attachment translate in the institutionalization and practice of diaspora giving.

I end this book by narrating how the idea for this project began. I turn to its origin story, so to speak, to show that diaspora giving, for me, has always been about the dreams, limitations, and ineffability of love. This book's dedication is to my late father, Manuel Mariano, a Filipino American immigrant who organized medical missions in the Philippines for the last eighteen years of his life. When I was still a college student, he would encourage me to join him on his trips to various provinces around Luzon, where he had arranged to provide medical, surgical, and sometimes emergency services to rural villages that may otherwise lack access to glaucoma surgeries, cataract implants, and other procedures related to the eye. Both my parents hail from the same barrio in Taytay, Rizal. My father entered the United States immediately following his graduation from medical school to continue his training and also with intentions to marry my mother, Lilia, who was working in Connecticut at the time. My parents were not voluntary Filipino immigrants to the United States. They did not intend to stay in the United States once my dad completed his residency, and in the family lore, they had even purchased their one-way return airplane tickets back to the Philippines, where they would live, work, and raise a family. The date of their return, however, was in the fall of 1972, the same week that Ferdinand Marcos declared martial law in the Philippines. The confusion of the initial days and weeks of martial law disrupted their plans, and my parents took measures to avoid the chaos and remain in the United States.

My father's life trajectory was again disrupted when at the relatively young age of forty-five, heart disease, cancer, and the onset of an autoimmune disease forced him into semiretirement, and he was no longer able to operate on patients. Though my dad was weak, he saw his poor health as a blessing that freed him from the obligations of his job at a hospital in North Dakota, where I was raised. His semiretirement gave him the time to organize annual medical missions in the Philippines that he carried out in conjunction with the North American Baptist Church. "Joyce, it was always my dream to be a missionary anyway," he would say to me when others saw his feeble health as a tragedy. Rather than bitter, he was grateful to be able not only to serve Filipinos but also to be near his family in the Philippines and to give my brothers and me opportunities to experience the Philippines while we were still young. It was important to my dad that we come to know the Philippines through experiences related to his linked values of nationalism, helping others, and evangelical proselytizing. Always with a joke and a smile, he teased relatives who would rather see us stay put in the family homes after our arrival in the Philippines, ideally, in their opinion, venturing out only to visit extended family, church, and the air-conditioned malls. Instead, we set out to provincial villages for the medical and surgical missions, the singular explanation my dad would give to friends in America for returning to the Philippines.

In my twenties, I took time off from college to join my parents on the first of several trips I made with medical missions to the Philippines to support my dad's efforts. I did not have any skills that would make me a useful contributor to these efforts; nor did I harbor any interest in pursuing a job in the medical field. I was there at the behest of my parents because they wanted to impart lessons about helping those less fortunate and to nurture a sense of being Filipino, especially for their American-born children, who had few other Filipino Americans with whom to socialize. Looking back and reflecting on the quiet moments with my dad when he would talk about the missions, I sense how helping others, giving back, home, homeland return, and being Filipino—all the concerns that propel this book—were intertwined in my memory, experience, and sense of both family and responsibility. At the same time, I can also see that my father's decades of distance from the Philippines, living in the United States, animated his dreams of helping poor Filipinos—returning, even if for just one or two months of the year, to a country that he once thought he had left behind.

I experienced profound feelings of isolation and cultural alienation on these mission trips with my parents in my college years, even as our various hosts went to enormous efforts to ensure that we were well fed, comfortable, and entertained. Unless given a specific task, I would keep to myself in the background of the commotion of hundreds of patients waiting to be treated by the dozen or so residents and helpers working with my father.

I interacted little with others, but I still carry a vivid memory of one particular midwife assistant, who worked at one of the rural hospitals where we stayed. She looked at me, filled with emotion, and told me over and over again how lucky I was that I lived in America, how she wished she could be me, and how fortunate I was that I had my mom and dad as parents. She wanted me to appreciate that my parents would care enough to bring me with them to the Philippines. I knew, of course, that she was referring not to me personally, as she hardly knew me, but to the vast differences between us in terms of education, opportunity, and material comforts. Why was she not lucky enough to be given the American dream?, she seemed to ask (at least, she did in my imagination). I knew that she was referring to my privilege, yet I was struggling to make sense of the contradictions that surrounded me during my stay in the Philippines. I did not share my parents' proselytizing values. I understood the American context of Protestantism and its history of colonization in the Philippines, but I did not know what it meant for me to go to the Philippines under the guise of missionary work. Another point of puzzlement for me was that white American missionaries accompanied us on the mission trips; as I understood it, my father's dream was to help the Philippines specifically as a Filipino returnee. I also remember struggling with my own sense of identity and how to be a good daughter without yielding my own nascent feminist and sexual politics. Alternatively, I felt self-indulgent for even having a crisis of identity, surrounded by reminders of my privilege, including the direct reminder from the midwife assistant.

It is not entirely far-fetched that I consider how my scholarly focus came about in response to those feelings of alienation, confusion, and contradiction. About a decade later, I began my doctoral research. My dad had died a few years earlier. In my fieldwork, I joined three different medical missions in the Philippines, including two in my parents' home province of Rizal. On one of those trips, I interviewed the medical director of a hospital who oversaw the *balikbayan* (returnee) medical missions in the vicinity. My aunt drove me to the hospital for the interview, and before leaving us to the meeting, my aunt asked the director about his plans to go to the United States. The director, a medical doctor, described his plans to work as a nurse at a hospital in Mississippi for a year and then move to Houston where he "had a connection." After one or two more years working in Houston, he hoped to eventually join a general practitioner's office as a doctor. I followed up on this conversation in the interview, and he spoke with deep resignation about his plans to leave. He knew that his leaving would contribute to a medical-care crisis in the Philippines, where there were already "far-flung areas where there are no doctors"—entire provincial hospitals that lacked a single full-time medical doctor. He commented on the lack of political will to address this crisis:

> There is a decreasing number of doctors, and the compensation really depends on your practice. The paying power of the people is decreased, so you turn to nursing [in the United States]. It's a sad fate, but what can we do? . . . It is a crisis in that it is a continual cycle until the government will respond. It's still economics. And the government hasn't responded yet. [Doctors] leaving the country [to work as nurses] increases the dollar and also the spending here, but it doesn't balance the health. The government is not conscious about the health care. What they care about is the dollar increasing. Maybe one day the government will wake up, and there will be no more doctors or nurses.[1]

It was not lost on me that here was a person whose current job as medical director of a provincial hospital put him in charge of overseeing Filipino American *balikbayan* doctors (like my father) on medical mission trips in the Philippines, telling me, a second-generation Filipino American, about his plan to work as a nurse in the United States, while Filipinos in the Philippines, by his own description, were in medical crisis. His comment that maybe one day there will be no doctors or nurses left in the Philippines because they were all compelled to find jobs in the United States conjured my somber yet unspoken reply: "Well, no doctors—save for the *balikbayans* here on medical missions." The medical doctor's fears, a soon-to-be-migrant's fears, dovetail with the diasporan's love.

My father returned to the Philippines and sometimes brought me with him because of his professed love for homeland and for family and as a Filipino, a U.S. citizen, a doctor, and a parent. This medical doctor of a Philippine hospital was hoping to go the United States for personal, economic reasons. In my, admittedly problematic, projection, I imagine that the young midwife assistant wished that she could be like me for both those reasons, commenting on my parents' love for the Philippines and her dream of America. As with any relationship, love—love of the motherland and love of humankind—is not enough. It is not enough if we do not consider the multiple economies in Filipino American diaspora giving. I offer this book as an entry point to those considerations.

Notes

Introduction

1. Jocelyn Alvarez [pseudonym], telephone interview by the author, April 2, 2009.

2. I reference Arjun Appadurai's work on the movement of global forces. See Arjun Appadurai, *Modernity at Large: Cultural Dimensions of Globalization* (Minneapolis: University of Minnesota Press, 1996).

3. See Peter Redfield and Erica Bornstein, "An Introduction to the Anthropology of Humanitarianism," in *Forces of Compassion: Humanitarianism between Ethics and Politics*, ed. Erica Bornstein and Peter Redfield (Santa Fe, NM: School for Advanced Research Press, 2010), 3–30.

4. On the cycles of large foundations and their unpredictability, see Erica Kohl-Arenas, *The Self-Help Myth: How Philanthropy Fails to Alleviate Poverty* (Berkeley: University of California Press, 2015).

5. Dovelyn Rannveig Agunias and Kathleen Newland, "Engaging the Asian Diaspora," *Issue in Brief: A Joint Series of the IOM Regional Office for Asia and the Pacific and the Migration Policy Institute* 7 (November 2012): 2.

6. Marcel Mauss, *The Gift: The Form and Reason for Exchange in Archaic Societies* (1925; repr., London: Routledge, 1990).

7. Ibid., 100, 101.

8. Ibid., 83.

9. Simone Bateman, "When Marcel Mauss's *Essai sur le don* Becomes *The Gift*: Variations on the Theme of Solidarity," *Theoretical Medicine and Bioethics* 37, no. 6 (2016): 454.

10. Mary Douglas, "Foreword: No Free Gifts," in *The Gift: The Form and Reason for Exchange in Archaic Societies*, by Marcel Mauss (London: Routledge, 1990), x.

11. Ibid., ix.

12. Philippine households received almost thirty billion dollars from immigrant and international migrant Filipinos in 2014. World Bank, *Migration and Remittances Factbook, 2016* (Washington, DC: World Bank, 2016), 12, https://openknowledge.worldbank.org/bitstream/handle/10986/23743/9781464803192.pdf.

13. This is a vast literature, and Rodriguez, Guevarra, and Parreñas are three important voices in the examination of labor, migration, and the Philippine state. See Robyn Magalit Rodriguez, *Migrants for Export: How the Philippine State Brokers Labor to the World* (Minneapolis: University of Minnesota Press, 2010); Anna Romina Guevarra, *Marketing Dreams, Manufacturing Heroes: The Transnational Labor Brokering of Filipino Workers* (New Brunswick, NJ: Rutgers University Press, 2010); Rhacel Salazar Parreñas, *Servants of Globalization: Women, Migration, and Domestic Work* (Stanford, CA: Stanford University Press, 2001); and Rhacel Salazar Parreñas, *The Force of Domesticity: Filipina Migrants and Globalization* (New York: New York University Press, 2008).

14. See Neferti Xina M. Tadiar, *Fantasy-Production: Sexual Economies and Other Philippine Consequences for the New World Order* (Manila: Ateneo de Manila University Press, 2004).

15. In this brief engagement with migration and the Philippines' remittance economy, I risk eliding the ways that the categories "Filipino American" and "Filipino labor migrant" function in Philippine culture and relate to state categories of migration. This is something I take up directly in Chapter 1. To clarify, the majority of remittances to the Philippines, as far as they are sent through official channels and can be traced by the Philippine government, are sent through U.S.-based banks and other remittance-processing bodies. Only 3 percent of overseas Filipino workers—migrants working on contract and maintaining Philippine citizenship—live in the United States, while 65 percent of Filipino permanent residents or expatriates are in the United States. Meanwhile, the Philippine national culture celebrates overseas Filipino labor migrants for their willingness to work abroad and send remittances. The fact that it is likely that Filipino Americans send the majority of remittances to family in the Philippines speaks to the Philippines' need to facilitate and control Filipinos' desire and willingness to work overseas. See Commission on Filipinos Overseas, "Stock Estimates of Overseas Filipinos," December 2013, https://cfo.gov.ph/wp-content/uploads/statistics/stock_estimate/2013-Stock-Estimate.xlsx; and Bangko Sentral ng Pilipinas, "Overseas Filipinos' Cash Remittances, by Country, by Source," 2016, http://www.bsp.gov.ph/statistics/spei_pub/Table%2011.pdf.

16. The Marcos government in 1982 required migrant workers to remit 50 to 80 percent of their earnings through authorized channels. This mandate

was later lifted. See Katherine Gibson and Julie Graham, "Situating Migrants in Theory: The Case of Filipino Migrant Contract Construction Workers," in *Filipinos in Global Migrations: At Home in the World?*, ed. Filomeno V. Aguilar Jr. (Quezon City: Philippine Migration Research Network and Philippine Social Science Council, 2002), 39.

17. Lydia Tanguilig [pseudonym], interview by the author, Minneapolis, MN, May 3, 2005.

18. This is not to say that there are no other ways to critique the Philippine culture of remittance giving. Even a report prepared for the Asian Development Bank rehearses a perceived undesirable effect of remittances. The authors describe a marked trend in the remittance literature on the Philippines that identifies excessive, consumer-driven practices resulting from international labor migration and remittance giving: "Remittances have been used mostly for excessive consumption, not to increase the productive capacity of the sending country. Migration also is said to have perpetuated a culture of dependence on remittances on the part of beneficiary families, as well as on the migrant sending country. Propped up by large inflows of remittances, governments might conveniently postpone needed structural reforms to put the macroeconomic house in order. The compensatory nature of remittances presents a moral hazard, or dependency syndrome, that could impede economic growth as recipients reduce their participation in productive endeavors. For those reasons, some researchers believe that unless governments are able to come up with policies that will induce migrants to invest productively, remittances are unlikely to be transformed into a significant source of capital for development." Asian Development Bank, *Enhancing the Efficiency of Overseas Filipino Workers Remittances* (Manila: Asian Development Bank, 2004), 7.

19. Geraldine Bigay [pseudonym], interview by the author, Atlanta, GA, March 28, 2006.

20. Ibid.

21. Several vernacular Bikol languages are indigenous to the Bicol region, and Bigay's issues with Tagalog stem from it being the basis for Filipino, the national language of the Philippines. Tagalog is one of several major regional languages in the islands. Historically, it is the language of the Manila area, the economic and political capital and former imperial center of the Philippines, which is of significance for Filipino language—with its foundation in Tagalog—rising to the status of lingua franca.

22. For discussions of intra-Filipino, language-based, and region-based stereotypes and measures of Filipinoness, see Rick Bonus, *Locating Filipino Americans: Ethnicity and the Cultural Politics of Space* (Philadelphia: Temple University Press, 2000); and Antonio P. Contreras, "Engaging the Language, Culture and Politics in the Philippine Homeland from the Imaginations of Selected Filipino-American Students at the University of Hawai'i," *Asia-Pacific Social Science Review* 10, no. 1 (2010): 127–141.

23. Robyn Magalit Rodriguez, "Toward a Critical Filipino Studies Approach to Philippine Migration," in *Filipino Studies: Palimpsests of Nation and Diaspora*, ed. Martin F. Manalansan IV and Augusto F. Espiritu (New York: New York University Press, 2016), 37.

24. See Eric Estuar Reyes, "American Developmentalism and Hierarchies of Difference in R. Zamora Linmark's Rolling the R's," *Journal of Asian American Studies* 10, no. 2 (2007): 117–140.

25. "U.S. Senator Albert J. Beveridge Speaks on the Philippine Question, U.S. Senate, Washington, D.C., January 9, 1900," UCLA Center for Chinese Studies, December 10, 2004, https://www.international.ucla.edu/ccs/article/18454.

26. Interestingly, the origins of the Veterans of Foreign Wars of the United States (VFW) can be traced to this same place and time. This nonprofit organization was founded when sick and wounded veterans of the Philippine-American War returned to find they lacked the means to seek treatment and assistance. Initially established by veterans to help fellow veterans, the VFW eventually helped build funding efforts for the Vietnam, Korean War, World War II, and Women in Military Service memorials but, ironically, not for the Philippine-American War, which is referred to on its website as "the Philippine Insurrection." According to its website, "The Veterans of Foreign Wars of the United States is a nonprofit veterans service organization comprised of eligible veterans and military service members from the active, guard and reserve forces. We trace our roots back to 1899 when veterans of the Spanish-American War (1898) and the Philippine Insurrection (1899–1902) founded local organizations to secure rights and benefits for their service. Many arrived home wounded or sick. There was no medical care or veterans' pension for them, and they were left to care for themselves. In their misery, some of these veterans banded together and formed organizations that would eventually band together and become known as the Veterans of Foreign Wars of the United States." Veterans of Foreign Wars, "Who We Are," https://www.vfw.org/about-us (accessed August 15, 2020).

27. "U.S. Senator Albert J. Beveridge Speaks."

28. Albert Beveridge, "March of the Flag," September 16, 1898, http://voicesofdemocracy.umd.edu/beveridge-march-of-the-flag-speech-text/.

29. See Paul A. Kramer, "Race-Making and Colonial Violence in the U.S. Empire: The Philippine-American War as Race War," *Diplomatic History* 30, no. 2 (2006): 169–210.

30. For an example of how scholars integrate an analysis of Beveridge to theorize the prominence of Asia in the production of the modern American nation, see David Palumbo-Liu, *Asian/American: Historical Crossings of a Racial Frontier* (Stanford, CA: Stanford University Press, 1999), 19.

31. For examples of research in the historical study of racial formation and American empire, which also draw on Beveridge, see Paul A. Kramer,

The Blood of Government: Race, Empire, the United States, and the Philippines (Chapel Hill: University of North Carolina Press, 2006), 1–3; Mae M. Ngai, *Impossible Subjects: Illegal Aliens and the Making of Modern America* (Princeton, NJ: Princeton University Press, 2004), 101; and Rick Baldoz, *The Third Asiatic Invasion: Empire and Migration in Filipino America, 1898–1946* (New York: New York University Press, 2011), 25–27.

32. For examples from Asian American studies, Filipino studies, and American empire studies that use Beveridge to underscore normative assumptions of race, gender, and sexuality in the justification of American empire or the mutual constitution of America in relation to the Philippines as its racialized, gendered, and sexualized other, see Kandice Chuh, *Imagine Otherwise: On Asian Americanist Critique* (Durham, NC: Duke University Press, 2003), 45–48; Martin Joseph Ponce, *Beyond the Nation: Diasporic Filipino Literature and Queer Reading* (New York: New York University Press, 2012), 31–33; Amy Kaplan, "Romancing the Empire," in *The Anarchy of Empire in the Making of U.S. Culture* (Cambridge, MA: Harvard University Press, 2002), 92–93; and Yen Le Espiritu, *Home Bound: Filipino American Lives across Cultures, Communities, and Countries* (Berkeley: University of California Press, 2003), 48–50.

33. Renato Constantino, *The Filipinos in the Philippines and Other Essays* (Quezon City: Malaya Books, 1966), 47.

34. Elsewhere, Constantino writes, "The transformation of the conqueror into the *altruistic benefactor* through the alchemy of colonial education was premised on the distortion and outright suppression of information regarding Philippine resistance to American rule and the atrocities committed by the American army to crush that resistance." Renato Constantino, *A History of the Philippines: From the Spanish Colonization to the Second World War* (New York: Monthly Review Press, 2008), 313 (emphasis added).

35. Gillian Hart, "Development Critiques in the 1990s: *Culs de Sac* and Promising Paths," *Progress in Human Geography* 25, no. 4 (2001): 650.

36. Nermeen Shaikh, "Interrogating Charity and the Benevolence of Empire," *Development* 50, no. 2 (2007): 84.

37. See Anne Boran, "Introduction," in *Poverty: Malaise of Development*, ed. Anne Boran (Chester, UK: University of Chester, 2010), 1.

38. The literature on diaspora development has exploded in the past three decades. A few examples include Barbara J. Merz, Peter F. Geithner, and Lincoln C. Chen, eds., *Diasporas and Development* (Cambridge, MA: Global Equity Initiative, Asia Center, Harvard University, 2007); Dina Ionescu, *Engaging Diasporas as Development Partners for Home and Destination Countries: Challenges for Policymakers* (Geneva, Switzerland: International Organization for Migration, 2006), https://www.iom.int/sites/default/files/our_work/ICP/IDM/MRS26.pdf; Kathleen Newland, Aaron Terrazas, and Roberto Munster, "Diaspora Philanthropy: Private Giving and Public Policy," September 2010, https://www.migrationpolicy.org/research/diaspora-philanthropy-private-giving-and

-public-policy; and Jennifer M. Brinkerhoff, "David and Goliath: Diaspora Organizations as Partners in the Development Industry," *Public Administration and Development* 31, no. 1 (2011): 37–49.

39. Sonia Plaza, "Call for Papers: International Conference on Diaspora for Development, July 13–14, 2009," *People Move* (blog), March 26, 2009, http://blogs.worldbank.org/peoplemove/call-for-papers-international-conference-on-diaspora-for-development.

40. Dilip Ratha, "Migrant Remittances," *World Bank Blogs*, June 20, 2008, https://blogs.worldbank.org/peoplemove/migrant-remittances.

41. "Diaspora-Driven Development," *The Guardian*, http://www.theguardian.com/global-development-professionals-network/diaspora-driven-development (accessed August 15, 2020).

42. U.S. Agency for International Development, "Partnering with USAID: Building Alliances for Sustainable Solutions," 2012, p. 2, https://www.usaid.gov/sites/default/files/documents/1880/Partnering_with_USAID_Diasporas%28GDF2012%29.pdf.

43. U.S. Agency for International Development, "USAID and Diaspora: Partners in Development," May 12, 2017, pp. 2–3, https://www.usaid.gov/GlobalDevLab/documents/usaid-and-diaspora-partners-development.

44. Aihwa Ong, *Neoliberalism as Exception: Mutations in Citizenship and Sovereignty* (Durham, NC: Duke University Press, 2007), 5.

45. Joan Roelofs, "The Third Sector as a Protective Layer for Capitalism," *Monthly Review* 47, no. 4 (1995), https://monthlyreviewarchives.org/index.php/mr/article/view/MR-047-04-1995-08_2.

46. Ibid.

47. Robert F. Arnove, "Introduction," in *Philanthropy and Cultural Imperialism: The Foundations at Home and Abroad*, ed. Robert F. Arnove (Boston: G. K. Hall, 1980), 4.

48. After the breakup of the Rockefellers' Standard Oil Trust, the Rockefeller Foundation used its own holdings to help protect oil monopolies for the Rockefeller's Standard Oil Companies. David Horowitz describes the "genius" of the foundation's architecture, infusing commercial interest in charitable form: "Forced to dispense huge resources to keep its status, it salvaged something from the situation by understanding that it had a unique opportunity for private interest to operate on the cultural, political and social life of the society. Suspicion and resistance are forestalled by the assumption that what is nonprofit is disinterested and what is charitable is beneficial." David Horowitz, "The Foundations: Charity Begins at Home," *Ramparts* 7 (April 1969): 41. In another example of the capitalist function of the nonprofit, when the Justice Department's Antitrust Division forced a group of New York banks in 1961 to get rid of their controlling shares in a major U.S. securities corporation, five Rockefeller-controlled purchasers picked up 20 percent of the shares, including the Rockefeller Institute (a nonprofit research institution), the Rockefeller

Brothers Fund (a charitable organization worth $860 million today), and Colonial Williamsburg (a living museum in Virginia).

49. See Arnove, "Introduction." See also Joan Roelofs, *Foundations and Public Policy: The Mask of Pluralism* (Albany: State University of New York Press, 2003).

50. Miranda Joseph, *Against the Romance of Community* (Minneapolis: University of Minnesota Press, 2002), 70.

51. Tadiar, *Fantasy-Production*, 4.

52. Ibid., 6.

53. Lawrence J. Friedman, "Philanthropy in America: Historicism and Its Discontents," in *Charity, Philanthropy, and Civility in American History*, ed. Lawrence J. Friedman and Mark D. McGarvie (Cambridge: Cambridge University Press, 2003), 2.

54. I gesture here to the seminal work of Amy Kaplan, "'Left Alone with America': The Absence of Empire in the Study of American Culture," in *Cultures of United States Imperialism*, ed. Amy Kaplan and Donald E. Pease (Durham, NC: Duke University Press, 1993), 11.

55. Lisa Lowe, *Immigrant Acts: On Asian American Cultural Politics* (Durham, NC: Duke University Press, 1996), 98.

56. See Erica Bornstein, *Disquieting Gifts: Humanitarianism in New Delhi* (Stanford, CA: Stanford University Press, 2012), 12.

57. Hart, "Development Critiques in the 1990s," 650.

58. Tadiar, *Fantasy-Production*, 127.

59. See Redfield and Bornstein, "An Introduction to the Anthropology of Humanitarianism," 3. See also Susan Koshy's discussion of "old" and "new" diasporas, which references the "shifting forms of capitalism" in determining modes of migration. Susan Koshy, "Introduction," in *Transnational South Asians: The Making of a Neo-diaspora*, ed. Susan Koshy and R. Radhakrishnan (New Delhi: Oxford University Press), 7.

60. See Eric J. Pido, *Migrant Returns: Manila, Development, and Transnational Connectivity* (Durham, NC: Duke University Press, 2017).

61. The Commission on Filipinos Overseas estimates that there are more than three times the number of overseas Filipinos in the United States than in Saudi Arabia, the country with the second highest number. "Overseas Filipinos," according to these statistics, refers to migration status—permanent, temporary, and irregular: "Filipino immigrants and legal permanent residents abroad, Filipino spouses of foreign nationals, Filipinos naturalized in their host country, Filipino dual citizens, and their descendants"; "land-based and sea-based Filipino workers, intra-company transferees, students, trainees, entrepreneurs, businessmen, traders and others whose stay abroad is six month[s] or more, and their accompanying dependents"; and "Filipinos who are not properly documented or without valid residence or work permits, or who may be overstaying in a foreign country." Commission on Filipinos Overseas, "Stock Estimates of Overseas Filipinos."

62. Shaikh, "Interrogating Charity and the Benevolence of Empire," 88.

63. Ibid., 87.

64. Isagani J. Sarmiento, *Re-building the Roots of a Nation: Beyond a Parrot's Mind* (Fairfield, CA: Crumbs Pishonet, 2002).

65. Ibid., 13.

66. Ibid., 14.

67. Ibid., 15–17.

68. See Patricia Mooney Nickel and Angela M. Eikenberry, "A Critique of the Discourse of Marketized Philanthropy," *American Behavioral Scientist* 52, no. 7 (2009): 974–989; and Patricia Mooney Nickel and Angela M. Eikenberry, "Philanthropy in an Era of Global Governance," in *Third Sector Research*, ed. Rupert Taylor (New York: Springer, 2010), 269–279. Other scholars who examine philanthropy, foundations, and giving make related arguments about focusing on social relations and the material conditions of poverty in our philanthropic imaginations in ways that are also useful in my thinking. See Susan A. Ostrander, "Legacy and Promise for Social Justice Funding: Charitable Foundations and Progressive Social Movements, Past and Present," in *Foundations for Social Change: Critical Perspectives on Philanthropy and Popular Movements*, ed. Daniel Faber and Deborah McCarthy (Lanham, MD: Rowman and Littlefield, 2005), 33–59; Kohl-Arenas, *The Self-Help Myth*; Katharyne Mitchell and Chris Lizotte, "The Grassroots and the Gift: Moral Authority, American Philanthropy, and Activism in Education," *Foucault Studies* 18 (October 2014): 66–89; Susan Brinn Hyatt, "From Citizen to Volunteer: Neoliberal Governance and the Erasure of Poverty," in *The New Poverty Studies: The Ethnography of Power, Politics, and Impoverished People in the United States*, ed. Judith Goode and Jeff Maskovsky (New York: New York University Press, 2001), 201–235; and the multiple authors in INCITE! Women of Color against Violence, ed., *The Revolution Will Not Be Funded: Beyond the Non-profit Industrial Complex* (Boston: South End Press, 2009). For a similar argument in regard to Haitians in the United States, their support of projects and causes in Haiti, and the way that neoliberalism and long-distance nationalism can obscure connections to poverty, see Nina Glick Schiller and Georges Fouron, "'I Am Not a Problem without a Solution': Poverty and Transnational Migration," in *The New Poverty Studies: The Ethnography of Power, Politics, and Impoverished People in the United States*, ed. Judith Goode and Jeff Maskovsky (New York: New York University Press, 2001), 321–363. While not writing directly about giving, Robyn Rodriguez's work on migration from the Philippines addresses a similar point in regard to remittances and neoliberal governance: "As remittance money flows into the Philippines to support and sustain Filipino families and communities, the state can reduce its expenditures for social goods. In effect, through labor brokerage, the state can mask the displacements and inequalities that are endemic to neoliberalism. The Philippines has developed a transnational migration apparatus, which serves as a veritable export-processing zone to facilitate

the out-migration of workers. What I call labor brokerage is an economic strategy by the neoliberal Philippine state through which it draws from its overseas' citizens earnings abroad to pay for its exorbitant debts." See Rodriguez, "Toward a Critical Filipino Studies Approach to Philippine Migration," 39.

69. Nickel and Eikenberry, "A Critique of the Discourse of Marketized Philanthropy," 976.

Chapter 1

1. I reference the title of Stanley Karnow's *In Our Image: America's Empire in the Philippines* (New York: Random House, 1989). Michael Salman gives a scathing critique of Stanley Karnow's book, emphasizing U.S. imperialism's success in transforming decades of colonial rule and conquest into a benevolent civilizing mission. The fact that Karnow's book won the Pulitzer Prize in 1990 for history writing speaks to the ideological pervasiveness and persistence of the trope of benevolence. Related to my own points about diaspora giving in the contemporary global context, Salman writes that Philippine culture is to blame for its own impoverishment and inability to embrace American values: "By reifying Philippine culture, Karnow once again elides all questions about power, conquest, colonialism as domination, the exploitation of labor, exploitation in international trade, or the limited life choices available in an impoverished economy. . . . Because Filipinos overseas often send money back to relatives in the Philippines, Karnow sees the explosion of Filipino migration and overseas contract labor as an exercise of mutual obligation among kin, rather than the practice of labor exploitation on an international scale and a flight from the Philippines' floundering economy. According to Karnow, when the migration is to the United States, it is part of the special attachment bred by a 'uniquely benign' colonialism." Michael Salman, "In Our Orientalist Imagination: Historiography and the Culture of Colonialism in the United States," *Radical History Review* 1991, no. 50 (1991): 229.

2. Model-minority stereotypes show that personhood for people of color in the United States is precarious and contingent. It is given when value, which in this case refers to economic contributions and middle-class status, is ascribed. Here, I draw on Lisa Marie Cacho, who explains that racial stereotypes such as model minority are "degrading because they link race to other categories of devaluation, just as race is redeemed when linked to other properties of personhood universalized as socially valuable." Lisa Marie Cacho, *Social Death: Racialized Rightlessness and the Criminalization of the Unprotected* (New York: New York University Press, 2012), 3.

3. See, for example, Anna Romina Guevarra's critique of Jose Antonio Vargas's positioning of himself as a good migrant subject in his activism and struggles against deportation. Anna Romina Guevarra, "The Legacy of Undesirability: Filipino TNTs, 'Irregular Migrants' and 'Outlaws' in the U.S. Cultural

Imaginary," in *Filipino Studies: Palimpsests of Nation and Diaspora*, ed. Martin F. Manalansan IV and Augusto F. Espiritu (New York: New York University Press, 2016), 355–374.

4. Quoted in George Wehrfritz, "Workers for the World," *Newsweek*, October 3, 2004, http://www.newsweek.com/workers-world-129447.

5. Lucy Mae San Pablo Burns, *Puro Arte: Filipinos on the Stages of Empire* (New York: New York University Press, 2013), 171 (emphasis added).

6. On contributionism, see Robyn Magalit Rodriguez, "Toward a Critical Filipino Studies Approach to Philippine Migration," in *Filipino Studies: Palimpsests of Nation and Diaspora*, ed. Martin F. Manalansan IV and Augusto F. Espiritu (New York: New York University Press, 2016), 37. Rodriguez builds her argument through engagement with the influential text by Oscar V. Campomanes, "New Formations of Asian American Studies and the Question of U.S. Imperialism," *positions* 5, no. 2 (1997): 523–550. See also Oscar V. Campomanes, "Filipinos in the United States and Their Literature of Exile," in *Discrepant Histories, Translocal Essays on Filipino Cultures*, ed. Vicente L. Rafael (Philadelphia: Temple University Press, 1995), 159–192. For other works that examine the consequences of the American dream, see Neferti Xina M. Tadiar, *Fantasy-Production: Sexual Economies and Other Philippine Consequences for the New World Order* (Manila: Ateneo de Manila University Press, 2004); and Dylan Rodriguez, *Suspended Apocalypse: White Supremacy, Genocide, and the Filipino Condition* (Minneapolis: University of Minnesota Press, 2010).

7. Pratt further explains, "The term 'contact' foregrounds the interactive, improvisational dimensions of imperial encounters so easily ignored or suppressed by accounts of conquest and domination told from the invader's perspective." Mary Louise Pratt, *Imperial Eyes: Travel Writing and Transculturation*, 2nd ed. (London: Routledge, 2008), 8.

8. The influence of Grace Hong and Roderick Ferguson's approach to comparative racializations is evident here. See Grace Kyungwon Hong and Roderick A. Ferguson, "Introduction," in *Strange Affinities: The Gender and Sexual Politics of Comparative Racialization*, ed. Grace Kyungwon Hong and Roderick A. Ferguson (Durham, NC: Duke University Press, 2011), 1–22.

9. "Good News for the Poor: A Conference on Diaspora Philanthropy by Overseas Filipinos" (handout with conference rationale and schedule), n.d., in the author's possession.

10. Ligaya Lindio-McGovern, "Neo-liberal Globalization in the Philippines: Its Impact on Filipino Women and Their Forms of Resistance," *Journal of Developing Societies* 23, no. 1 (2007): 15.

11. With the idea of the projected image of their communion, I reference Benedict Anderson, *Imagined Communities: Reflections on the Origin and Spread of Nationalism*, rev. ed. (New York: Verso, 1991).

12. Lisa Marie Cacho, "Racialized Hauntings of the Devalued Dead," in *Strange Affinities: The Gender and Sexual Politics of Comparative Racialization*,

ed. Grace Kyungwon Hong and Roderick A. Ferguson (Durham, NC: Duke University Press, 2011), 41.

13. See the Save a Tahanan home page, at http://save-a-tahanan.org/sti_index.php.

14. Feed The Hungry, "Mission" (brochure), n.d., in the author's possession.

15. See Commission on Filipinos Overseas, "Stock Estimates of Overseas Filipinos," December 2013, https://cfo.gov.ph/wp-content/uploads/statistics/stock_estimate/2013-Stock-Estimate.xlsx.

16. Denise Cruz, *Transpacific Femininities: The Making of the Modern Filipina* (Durham, NC: Duke University Press, 2012), 7.

17. Khachig Tölölyan, "The Contemporary Discourse of Diaspora Studies," *Comparative Studies of South Asia, Africa and the Middle East* 27, no. 3 (2007): 649.

18. Filomeno V. Aguilar, "Beyond Stereotypes: Human Subjectivity in the Structuring of Global Migrations," in *At Home in the World? Filipinos in Global Migrations*, ed. Filomeno V. Aguilar (Quezon City: Philippine Migration Research Network and Philippine Social Science Council, 2002), 17.

19. Benito M. Vergara Jr., *Pinoy Capital: The Filipino Nation in Daly City* (Philadelphia: Temple University Press, 2009), 45.

20. Ibid., 135 (emphasis in original).

21. Ibid., 5.

22. Wehrfritz, "Workers for the World."

23. E. San Juan Jr., "Overseas Filipino Workers: The Making of an Asian-Pacific Diaspora," *Global South* 3, no. 2 (2009): 99.

24. Maruja M. B. Asis, "The Philippines' Culture of Migration," January 1, 2006, http://www.migrationinformation.org/USFocus/display.cfm?ID=364.

25. See Commission on Filipinos Overseas, "Stock Estimates of Overseas Filipinos."

26. San Juan, "Overseas Filipino Workers," 100.

27. Of the approximately ten million overseas Filipinos counted by the CFO, 48 percent (4,869,766) are permanent residents of countries other than the Philippines. Of this 48 percent, the majority are permanent residents of the United States (3,135,293). See Commission on Filipinos Overseas, "Stock Estimates of Overseas Filipinos."

28. While the statistics on remittances to the Philippines are difficult to track, of the almost $16.5 billion in remittances that entered the Philippines through traceable channels, almost $8 billion came from the United States in 2008. See Bangko Sentral ng Pilipinas, "Overseas Filipinos' Cash Remittances, by Country, by Source," 2016, http://www.bsp.gov.ph/statistics/spei_pub/Table%2011.pdf.

29. Anna Romina Guevarra, *Marketing Dreams, Manufacturing Heroes: The Transnational Labor Brokering of Filipino Workers* (New Brunswick, NJ: Rutgers University Press, 2010), 171 (emphasis added).

30. Ibid., 161 (emphasis in original).

31. Ibid., 161, 111–112.

32. Tadiar, *Fantasy-Production*, 28.

33. Caroline S. Hau, *On the Subject of the Nation: Filipino Writings from the Margins, 1981–2004* (Quezon City: Ateneo de Manila University Press, 2004), 236.

34. Vicente L. Rafael, *White Love and Other Events in Filipino History* (Durham, NC: Duke University Press, 2000), 208.

35. See Catherine Ceniza Choy, *Empire of Care: Nursing and Migration in Filipino American History* (Durham, NC: Duke University Press, 2003), 191.

36. Hau, *On the Subject of the Nation*, 237.

37. Jose M. Montelibano, "Glimpses: The $8 Billion Fil-Am Remittance," *Philippine Daily Inquirer*, August 20, 2010 (emphasis added).

38. See the Bagong Bayani Foundation home page, at https://www.bbfi.com.ph/#home.

39. Bagong Bayani Foundation, "Awards Criteria," https://www.bbfi.com.ph/files/criteria.php (accessed September 25, 2020).

40. Ibid.

41. "Compassion of 4 Filipino Caregivers during Japan Tragedy Cited," *SunStar Manila*, April 19, 2012.

42. Ibid.

43. Commission on Filipinos Overseas, "Primer" (brochure), 2009, in the author's possession.

44. The text of the policy, Executive Order No. 498 (December 19, 1991), is available at https://www.officialgazette.gov.ph/1991/12/19/executive-order-no-498-s-1991/.

45. Commission on Filipinos Overseas, "Presidential Awards for Filipino Individuals and Organizations Overseas," https://www.presidentialawards.cfo.gov.ph (accessed September 25, 2020).

46. Antoinette R. Raquiza, "Changing Configuration of Philippine Capitalism," *Philippine Political Science Journal* 35, no. 2 (2014): 230.

47. Ibid.

48. Burns, *Puro Arte*, 80.

49. Jose Aspiras, "Tourism in 1973 . . . a Success All the Way," quoted in Linda K. Richter, "The Philippines: The Politicization of Tourism," in *The Sociology of Tourism: Theoretical and Empirical Investigations*, ed. Yiorgos Apostolopoulos, Stella Leivadi, and Andrew Yiannakis (London: Routledge, 1996), 235.

50. Angelo Alaan [pseudonym], interview by the author, San Francisco, CA, April 4, 2005.

51. Joseph Pimentel, "Bucks from the Big Box," *Asian Journal MDWK Magazine*, September 18–19, 2008, p. 3.

52. Georgie Cruz [pseudonym], interview by the author, Makati, Philippines, May 19, 2005.

53. Quoted in Jeremaiah Opiniano, "Overseas Migration: A Filipino 'Fixture' Forms a Nation's Future," *Pacific Rim Report*, no. 47 (August 2007), https://www.usfca.edu/sites/default/files/pdfs/report-47.pdf.

54. The Angeleños in Southern California website, from which this quotation was taken, is no longer functional.

55. Hilario Gonzales [pseudonym], interview by the author, Los Angeles, CA, September 25, 2005.

56. This mandate was introduced by President Marcos in December 1982 through Executive Order Number 857. See Katherine Gibson and Julie Graham, "Situating Migrants in Theory: The Case of Filipino Migrant Contract Construction Workers," in *Filipinos in Global Migrations: At Home in the World?*, ed. Filomeno V. Aguilar Jr. (Quezon City: Philippine Migration Research Network and Philippine Social Science Council, 2002), 39; and Asian Development Bank, *Enhancing the Efficiency of Overseas Filipino Workers Remittances* (Manila: Asian Development Bank, 2004), 47.

57. Quoted in Guevarra, *Marketing Dreams, Manufacturing*, 3. See also Steven C. McKay, "Filipino Sea Men: Identity and Masculinity in a Global Labor Niche," in *Asian Diasporas: New Formations, New Conceptions*, ed. Rhacel Salazar Parreñas and Lok C. D. Siu (Stanford, CA: Stanford University Press, 2007), 72; Robyn Magalit Rodriguez, *Migrants for Export: How the Philippine State Brokers Labor to the World* (Minneapolis: University of Minnesota Press, 2010), 84; and Kale Bantigue Fajardo, *Filipino Crosscurrents: Oceanographies of Seafaring, Masculinities, and Globalization* (Minneapolis: University of Minnesota Press, 2011), 80–86.

58. Shu-Ju Ada Cheng, *Serving the Household and the Nation: Filipina Domestics and the Politics of Identity in Taiwan* (Lanham, MD: Lexington Books, 2006), 32.

59. Rodriguez, *Migrants for Export*, 12.

60. Walden Bello, Herbert Docena, Marissa de Guzman, and Marylou Malig, *The Anti-development State: The Political Economy of Permanent Crisis in the Philippines* (Quezon City: University of the Philippines Department of Sociology and Focus on the Global South, 2004), 11.

61. Quoted in Wehrfritz, "Workers for the World."

62. Tina Santos [pseudonym], interview by the author, Manila, Philippines, January 5, 2004.

63. David L. Eng, *Racial Castration: Managing Masculinity in Asian America* (Durham, NC: Duke University Press, 2001), 2.

Chapter 2

1. Rosca does not identify as Filipino American but as a transnational Filipina. When referring to Rosca's own self-expressed identity and politics, I

refrain from using the term "Filipino American." I interviewed Rosca over several sessions that took place in Honolulu and New York City in 2015.

2. Johanna Brenner, "Feminism's March from Nation to Home—an Interview with Ninotchka Rosca," *Against the Current* 163 (March–April 2013): 16. See also Braden Goyette, "Interview with Ninotchka Rosca," *Maisonneuve*, May 16, 2010, http://maisonneuve.org/article/2010/05/16/interview-ninotchka-rosca; and Anna Romina Guevarra, *Marketing Dreams, Manufacturing Heroes: The Transnational Labor Brokering of Filipino Workers* (New Brunswick, NJ: Rutgers University Press, 2010).

3. See Nermeen Shaikh, "Interrogating Charity and the Benevolence of Empire," *Development* 50, no. 2 (2007): 87.

4. Arif Dirlik, "Developmentalism: A Critique," *Interventions* 16, no. 1 (2012): 30–31 (emphasis added).

5. The quote is attributed to Marcos in his nationwide announcement of martial law. Quoted in Jose V. Fuentecilla, *Fighting from a Distance: How Filipino Exiles Helped Topple a Dictator* (Urbana: University of Illinois Press, 2013), 1.

6. P. N. Abinales, "The Post-Marcos Regime, the Non-bourgeois Opposition and the Prospects of a Philippine 'October,'" *Kasarinlan: Philippine Journal of Third World Studies* 1, no. 4 (1986): 37.

7. Quoted in Marco Cuevas-Hewitt, "The Figure of the 'Fil-Whatever': Filipino American Trans-Pacific Social Movements and the Rise of Radical Cosmopolitanism," *World Anthropologies Network E-Journal* 5 (July 2010): 102, http://www.ram-wan.net/old/documents/05_e_Journal/journal-5/6-cuevas.pdf. There is currently an exciting wave of work being published on the KDP, which has begun to shift our understanding of the significance of this organization. Scholars such as Joy Sales, Mark Sanchez, and Karen Buenavista Hanna all contribute to this moment. See their respective chapters in Robyn Magalit Rodriguez, ed., *Filipino American Transnational Activism: Diasporic Politics among the Second Generation* (Leiden, Netherlands: Brill, 2020).

8. Helen C. Toribio, "We Are Revolution: A Reflective History of the Union of Democratic Filipinos (KDP)," *Amerasia Journal* 24, no. 2 (1998): 177n12.

9. Cuevas-Hewitt, "The Figure of the 'Fil-Whatever,'" 105.

10. CPP materials, quoted in Augusto Espiritu, "Journeys of Discovery and Difference: Transnational Politics and the Union of Democratic Filipinos," in *The Transnational Politics of Asian Americans*, ed. Christian Collet and Pei-te Lien (Philadelphia: Temple University Press, 2009), 44.

11. Ibid.

12. Benjamin Pimentel, "Defying Marcos, Filipino Americans Emerged as a Force against Tyranny," *Philippine Daily Inquirer*, September 18, 2012, http://globalnation.inquirer.net/50480/defying-marcos-filipino-americans-emerged-as-a-force-against-tyranny.

13. Gillian Hart, "Development Critiques in the 1990s: *Culs de Sac* and Promising Paths," *Progress in Human Geography* 25, no. 4 (2001): 650.

14. See Richard Sandbrook, "Globalization and the Limits of Neoliberal Development Doctrine," *Third World Quarterly* 21, no. 6 (2000): 1071–1080.

15. Anne Boran, "Introduction," in *Poverty: Malaise of Development*, ed. Anne Boran (Chester, UK: University of Chester, 2010), 27.

16. "Filipino-Americans Aim to Revitalize Homeland," *New York Times*, April 20, 1986, https://www.nytimes.com/1986/04/20/nyregion/filipino-americans-aim-to-revitalize-homeland.html.

17. See Jodi Kim, "An 'Orphan' with Two Mothers: Transnational and Transracial Adoption, the Cold War, and Contemporary Asian American Cultural Politics," *American Quarterly* 61, no. 4 (2009): 860.

18. For information on the post-Marcos Philippines, see the special issue of *Kasarinlan: Philippine Journal of Third World Studies* 1, no. 4 (1986). Several articles from that issue are cited in this chapter.

19. See IBON Databank Staff, "High Hopes amidst a Wasted Legacy," *Kasarinlan: Philippine Journal of Third World Studies* 1, no. 4 (1986): 7–12.

20. William Safran, "Diasporas in Modern Societies: Myths of Homeland and Return," *Diaspora: A Journal of Transnational Studies* 1, no. 1 (1991): 85, 83.

21. Ibid., 83, 84.

22. Lily Cho, "The Turn to Diaspora," *TOPIA: Canadian Journal of Cultural Studies* 17 (2007): 14 (emphasis in original).

23. Ibid., 12.

24. Martin F. Manalansan IV, "Beyond Authenticity: Rerouting the Filipino Culinary Diaspora," in *Eating Asian America: A Food Studies Reader*, ed. Robert Ji-Song Ku, Martin F. Manalansan IV, and Anita Mannur (New York: New York University Press, 2013), 291.

25. Aurélie Bouzerda-Wahlen, Louis Nahum, Radek Ptak, and Armin Schnider, "Mechanism of Disorientation: Reality Filtering versus Content Monitoring," *Cortex* 49 (2013): 2628. See also Gary R. VanderBos, *APA Dictionary of Psychology*, 2nd ed. (Washington, DC: American Psychological Association, 2015).

26. Lucy Yardley, "Understanding Embodied Experience," in *Qualitative Health Psychology: Theories and Methods*, ed. Michael Murray and Kerry Chamberlain (London: Sage, 1999), 41.

27. Bouzerda-Wahlen et al., "Mechanism of Disorientation," 2629. The *APA Dictionary of Psychology* defines disorientation as "impaired ability to identify oneself or to locate oneself in relation to time, place, or other aspects of one's surroundings." See VanderBos, *APA Dictionary of Psychology*, 323.

28. Ninotchka Rosca, interview by the author, Honolulu, March 20, 2015.

29. Brenner, "Feminism's March from Nation to Home."

30. Rosca, interview by the author.

31. Brenner, "Feminism's March from Nation to Home."

32. Rosca, interview by the author.

33. Ninotchka Rosca, "The Day Manila Fell Silent," *Doveglion Lit*, September 12, 2012, https://doveglionlit.wordpress.com/2012/09/12/ninotchka-rosca-the-day-manila-fell-silent.

34. See Kandice Chuh, *Imagine Otherwise: On Asian Americanist Critique* (Durham, NC: Duke University Press, 2003), 86–87.

35. Ibid., 87.

36. Mimi Thi Nguyen, *The Gift of Freedom: War, Debt, and Other Refugee Passages* (Durham, NC: Duke University Press, 2012), 25.

Chapter 3

1. See the organization's home page, at http://www.phildev.org/.

2. Ibid.

3. Ibid.

4. PhilDev, "Our Story," http://www.phildev.org/our-story/ (accessed August 15, 2020).

5. In 1961, Ayala established what would become the Ayala Foundation, but its "earliest social commitment was made in education with the creation of La Concordia, a school for girls, in 1856." It describes its "seeds of social involvement" in *Ayala at 175*, a special print magazine published by Ayala to commemorate its 175th anniversary: "In 1856, Margarita [Roxas de Ayala] . . . donated her estate in Paco in Sta. Ana, Manila to the Sisters of Charity, [which] would soon be converted into a girls' school—the Colegio de la Inmaculada Concepcion de la Concordia." Sarge Lacuesta, *Ayala at 175* (Makati, Philippines: Ayala Corporation, 2009), 9, https://issuu.com/accomm/docs/ayala_at_175_mag.

6. For example, see Ayala, "Sustaining CSR in Difficult Times: Jaime Agusto Zobel de Ayala's Speech at the Asian Forum on Corporate Social Responsibility," November 19, 2009, https://www.ayala.com.ph/press-room/press-releases/sustaining-csr-difficult-times-jaime-augusto-zobel-de-ayalas-speech-asian. Representatives of Ayala continue to win awards for corporate responsibility and sustainability. The company received recognition from the Asia Corporate Excellence and Sustainability Awards, the ASEAN Corporate Sustainability Summit and Awards, CMO Asia Best CSR Practices Awards, and the Asian CSR Award for Environment and Value Chain Management. See Ayala, "Awards," http://www.ayala.com.ph/awards (accessed August 15, 2020).

7. Synergos, "Q & A with Jaime Augusto Zobel de Ayala II," 2003, https://www.synergos.org/news-and-insights/2003/q-jaime-augusto-zobel-de-ayala-ii.

8. Stacey Choe and Madhurya Manohar, "ASEAN Impact 25: Impactful Philanthropists in ASEAN," 2018, https://asiaphilanthropycircle.org/asean-impact-25-impactful-philanthropists-in-asean/.

9. Ibid. In addition to the figureheads, Ayala's organization materials have consistently, almost sixty years since the family group established its corporate

foundation in the Philippines, worked to present its evolving frameworks of social development and social responsibility: "In the past, the foundation's mission was to contribute to the eradication of various forms of poverty in the country; today, it has chosen a strategic, integrated, and sustainable approach to poverty alleviation by focusing on the needs and aspirations of specific communities." Ayala Foundation, "Frequently Asked Questions," http://www.ayalafoundation.org/faq/ (accessed August 15, 2020).

10. Simon Zadek, *The Civil Corporation: The New Economy of Corporate Citizenship* (Sterling, VA: Earthscan, 2001), 55.

11. See Clay Westcott and Jennifer Brinkerhoff, eds., *Converting Migration Drains into Gains: Harnessing the Resources of Overseas Professionals* (Manila: Asian Development Bank, 2006); and Victoria P. Garchitorena, "Diaspora Philanthropy: The Philippine Experience," May 2007, https://www.cbd.int/financial/charity/philippines-diaspora.pdf.

12. For a view of Garchitorena's presentation to the United Nations Institute for Training and Research, see Victoria P. Garchitorena, *Migration and Development: Philippine Diaspora Philanthropy* (New York: United Nations Institute for Training and Research, 2007).

13. Ayala, "2019 Integrated Report," April 2020, p. 61, https://ayala.com.ph/sites/default/files/pdfs/Ayala%20Corp%202019%20Integrated%20Report.pdf.

14. Ibid., 217, 222.

15. According to its 2019 annual report, the net earnings of the Bank of the Philippines "jumped 25 percent" from 2018 to ₱28.8 billion, "investment properties expanded 8 percent to ₱246.7 billion," "the property development business generated ₱117.6 billion in revenues," and "the shopping centers segment, represented by Ayala Malls, posted revenues of ₱22.0 billion, 11 percent higher than previous year." Ibid., 221, 222, 129, 130.

16. Justin Doebele, "Philippines 40 Richest," *Forbes*, December 15, 2006, https://www.forbes.com/global/2006/1225/039.html#5f3ae9fd300f.

17. "Philippines' 50 Richest," *Forbes*, 2020, https://www.forbes.com/philippines-billionaires/list/. See also Antoinette R. Raquiza, "Changing Configuration of Philippine Capitalism," *Philippine Political Science Journal* 35, no. 2 (2014): 225–250.

18. See Joshua Barkan, *Corporate Sovereignty: Law and Government under Capitalism* (Minneapolis: University of Minnesota Press, 2013), 111. Barkan writes, "As early as the 1960s and 1970s, activists, politicians, lawmakers, diplomats, academics, and corporate marketing departments were generating new visions of corporate capitalism, its regulatory frameworks, and its social duties, obligations, and privileges. By the 1990s, responsibility and citizenship had moved from debated terms to semiformal, quasi-legal regulatory regimes, coalescing into corporate social responsibility (CSR) and corporate citizenship" (111).

19. Ibid., 113.

20. Choe and Manohar, "ASEAN Impact 25," 63.

21. "Fil-Ams Exhorted to Help Philippines," *Filipino Reporter* 28, no. 42 (2000): 1.

22. See Stuart Hall, "Cultural Identity and Diaspora," in *Identity: Community, Culture, Difference*, ed. Jonathan Rutherford (London: Lawrence and Wishart, 1990), 222–237; and Stuart Hall, "Notes on Deconstructing 'the Popular,'" in *People's History and Socialist Theory*, ed. Raphael Samuel (London: Routledge and Kegan Paul, 1981), 227–240.

23. See Robert Biel, "Critical Perspectives on Issues of Global Poverty," in *Poverty: Malaise of Development*, ed. Anne Boran (Chester, UK: Chester Academic Press, 2010), 66–92.

24. See Iris Marion Young, *Responsibility for Justice* (New York: Oxford University Press, 2010), esp. chaps. 4–5.

25. Ibid., 95.

26. Ibid.

27. See "Ayala Foundation USA Hosts Gala to Inaugurate Transformation to PhilDev USA," *Business Wire*, September 3, 2010, https://www.businesswire.com/news/home/20100903005144/en/Ayala-Foundation-USA-Hosts-Gala-Inaugurate-Transformation.

28. Tony Acoba [pseudonym], interview by the author, Makati, Philippines, June 17, 2005.

29. See Linda Basch, Nina Glick Schiller, and Christina Szanton Blanc, *Nations Unbound: Transnational Project, Postcolonial Predicaments, and Deterritorialized Nation-States* (New York: Gordon and Breach Science, 2000), 30.

30. Nancy Fraser, "Reframing Justice in a Globalizing World," *New Left Review* 36 (November–December 2005): 12.

31. Ibid.

32. James K. Rowe, "Corporate Social Responsibility as Business Strategy," UC Santa Cruz Center for Global, International and Regional Studies, 2005, https://escholarship.org/uc/item/5dq43315 (emphasis in original).

33. Diosdado P. Banatao, "Chairman's Message," in *Ayala Foundation USA Annual Report, 2008* (Redwood City, CA: Ayala Foundation USA), 5.

34. Neferti Xina M. Tadiar, *Fantasy-Production: Sexual Economies and Other Philippine Consequences for the New World Order* (Manila: Ateneo de Manila University Press, 2004), 6.

35. Ibid., 4.

36. Ibid., 7. Earlier in the introduction, Tadiar writes, "When I speak of dreams, I use the term loosely to indicate that our actions are also wishes, the expression of which is constrained by the unconscious or, more accurately, imaginary structures and logics of organization of our material realities. In my usage, fantasies are the hegemonic forms of expression of our desiring-actions. Dreams are the concrete work of imagination while fantasies are the abstract forms into which this work becomes subsumed within the world-system of

production. Fantasies are, on this view, alienated means of production, while the desiring-actions in dreams are living labour" (6).

37. Ibid., 38.

38. See Kenji Koike, "The Ayala Group during the Aquino Period: Diversification along with a Changing Ownership and Management Structure," *Developing Economies* 31, no. 4 (1993): 444–445.

39. Miranda Joseph, *Against the Romance of Community* (Minneapolis: University of Minnesota Press, 2002), 70.

40. Ibid., xxiv.

41. Synergos, "Q & A with Jaime Augusto Zobel de Ayala II."

42. Quoted in Jane Nelson and Caroline Bergrem, "Values and Value: Communicating the Strategic Importance of Corporate Citizenship to Investors," World Economic Forum and the Prince of Wales International Business Leaders Forum, 2004, p. 29, https://docplayer.net/96430975-Values-and-value-communicating-the-strategic-importance-of-corporate-citizenship-to-investors.html.

43. Tadiar, *Fantasy-Production*, 127.

44. Mariel Q. de Jesus, "Can Business 'Do Good' in Bad Times?," *Philippine Daily Inquirer*, January 17, 2009.

45. Ayala, "About," https://ayala.com.ph/about-ayala (accessed October 1, 2020).

46. Jean Comaroff and John L. Comaroff, "Millennial Capitalism: First Thoughts on a Second Coming," *Public Culture* 12, no. 2 (2000): 292.

47. Ayala Foundation USA, *AF-USA e-Bulletin* 4, no. 1 (January 2005).

48. Jaime Augusto Zobel de Ayala II, "The Challenges of Asian Philanthropy in the 21st Century," speech given at Worldwide Initiatives for Grantmaker Support "Making a Difference in Philanthropy" conference, November 16, 2006, Bangkok.

49. Fernando Zobel de Ayala, "Enlightened Capitalism towards a More Sustainable Future," *PhilStar Global*, November 20, 2009, https://www.philstar.com/business/2009/11/20/524531/enlightened-capitalism-towards-more-sustainable-future.

50. To implicate the government of the Philippines in this relationship and to extend my interpretation of Zobel de Ayala's discussion of natural disasters and capitalism's responsibility for human suffering, consider that the Philippine government was aware of pending landslides caused by irresponsible deforestation and corporate "environmental predators." Though aware of pending disaster, the government failed to warn the village of Guinsaugon of the instability of its environment. It was estimated that more than one thousand people were buried in the mudslide. See Carlos H. Conde, "Dangers of Philippine Landslides Often Ignored, Critics Say," *New York Times*, February 21, 2006, https://www.nytimes.com/2006/02/21/world/asia/danger-of-philippine-landslides-often-ignored-critics-say.html.

51. Michael Blowfield, "Corporate Social Responsibility: Reinventing the Meaning of Development?," in "Critical Perspectives on Corporate Social Responsibility," special issue of *International Affairs* 81, no. 3 (2005): 520.

52. J. Robbie Fabian, "Ayala Foundation USA Pre-marketing Study: Research on the Philanthropic Patterns and Inclinations of Filipino Americans," n.d., in the author's possession.

53. Ibid., 4.

54. In a different context, Arlene Dávila works to historicize the "truth" of the Latin American market in the United States with a critique of the relationship between the "Hispanic market" and dominant definitions of Latinidad: "I start from the premise that the reconstitution of individuals into consumers and populations into markets are central fields of cultural production that reverberate within public understanding of people's place, and hence of their rights and entitlements, in a given society. Looking at Hispanic marketing is therefore particularly revealing of the relationship between culture, corporate sponsorship, and politics, and moreover can illuminate how commercial representations may shape people's cultural identities as well as affect notions of belonging and cultural citizenship in public life." See Arlene Dávila, *Latinos Inc.: Marketing and the Making of a People* (Berkeley: University of California Press, 2012), 2. While her work deconstructs the mobilization of corporate-defined racial categories within the racial/ethnic hierarchies and landscape of the United States—Latinos have "come of age" because advertising is paying attention—this is quite different from the use of the "Filipino American market" by the Ayala Foundation. The Ayala Foundation does homogenize the Filipino American market as people who have "made it" economically, erasing continued racial and ethnic discrimination and economic disparities. However, its marketing campaigns stay largely outside mainstream venues and, hence, outside the discourse on "celebrations" of diversity.

55. After Marcos imposed martial law in 1972, the government launched a massive attack on the communist New People's Army, forcing more than fifty thousand people into concentration camps. Guerrilla warfare units of the New People's Army ignited a radical response of national democracy among students, the church, and peasants, resulting in what is referred to as the First Quarter Storm of 1972. See Dev Nathan, "Armed Struggle in Philippines," *Economic and Political Weekly* 22, no. 51 (1987): 2201.

56. Gisela Velasco, *Corporate Philanthropy in Asia: The Philippine Case; An Overview of East and Southeast Asian Philanthropy* (New York: Center on Philanthropy and Civil Society, CUNY Graduate Center, 1996), 14.

57. See M. Todd Henderson and Malani Anup, "Corporate Philanthropy and the Market for Altruism," *Columbia Law Review* 109 (2009): 578.

58. The quotation is attributed to Jaime Augusto Zobel de Ayala in Nic Legaspi, "CEOs' Views on CSR: Business Is a Two-Way Street," *BizNews Asia* 2, no. 20 (2004): 16 (emphasis added).

59. See Blowfield, "Corporate Social Responsibility," 515–524.

60. Acoba, interview by the author. Acoba was at the time of the interview a project manager of the Ayala Foundation. His description of the shift in funding is echoed by Gisela Velasco: "A major cause of concern among NGOs nowadays is the issue of sustaining the work that has flourished in the face of declining foreign assistance. It should be noted that the majority of the support for all social development work came from overseas assistance. . . . The size of this funding dramatically rose during the Corazon Aquino government and led to a rapid increase in the number of NGOs. As the country moved from the dark days of repression and the glorious days of democratic uprising, donors shifted their attention to other countries in Eastern Europe and Africa. The problem of over-dependence on external funds has prompted some forward-looking NGOs to start building other sources of funding through endowments and investment management, undertaking business ventures and providing fee-based technical services." See Velasco, *Corporate Philanthropy in Asia*, 9.

61. Ayala Foundation USA, "Guidelines for Partnership," n.d., in the author's possession.

62. Joseph, *Against the Romance of Community*, 70, vii–xi.

63. Rowe, "Corporate Social Responsibility as Business Strategy," 4.

64. Jaime Augusto Zobel de Ayala (chairman and CEO of the board of Ayala and co–vice chairman of the board for the Ayala Foundation), quoted in Doreen Yu, "Ayala on Solid Ground after 175 Years," *PhilStar Global*, March 9, 2009, https://www.philstar.com//2009/03/09/446608/ayala-solid-ground-after-175-years.

65. Portions of the organization's former home page are available at https://www.guidestar.org/profile/94-3369973.

66. Ibid.

67. Benito M. Vergara Jr., "Betrayal, Class Fantasies, and the Filipino Nation in Daly City," *Philippine Sociological Review* 44, no. 1–4 (1996): 143.

68. Ayala Foundation USA, "Ayala Foundation USA Donation Process" (brochure), n.d., in the author's possession.

69. Ayala Foundation USA, "Guidelines for Partnership."

70. According the Philippine Council for NGO Certification (PCNC) website, "When it started operations in 1999, the original mission of PCNC was to be the pre-eminent certifying body of Philippine NGOs aspiring for 'donee institution status' issued by the Bureau of Internal Revenue (BIR). Starting 2009, or 10 years after, PCNC expanded its mission to improving the effectiveness of 'Philippine NGOs so that they become increasingly accountable, credible and capable in providing services to those in need and to be instrumental in creating a culture of giving.'" Philippine Council for NGO Certification, "About Us," https://www.pcnc.com.ph/about/ (accessed October 1, 2020). For an elaboration of the nonprofit industrial complex, see INCITE! Women of Color against Violence, ed., *The Revolution Will Not Be Funded: Beyond the Non-profit Industrial Complex* (Boston: South End Press, 2009).

71. Acoba, interview by the author.

72. For example, the Ayala Foundation believes that the "most saleable," to quote Tony Acoba, projects are "projects about education and about health. From donating secondhand medical equipment to rural health units in the Philippines, to donating actual cash for health programs like health-related programs like feeding program for malnourished children." See ibid.

73. See what Catherine E. Walsh refers to as "neoliberal multiculturalism" such that the "cultural logic of global capitalism comes to serve as a modern-day form of colonization that obfuscates and at the same time maintains the colonial difference through the discursive rhetoric of multiculturalism." Catherine E. Walsh, "The (Re)Articulation of Political Subjectivities and Colonial Difference in Ecuador: Reflections on Capitalism and the Geopolitics of Knowledge," *Nepantla: Views from the South* 3, no. 1 (2002): 83.

74. Mario Deriquito, paper presented at "Good News for the Poor: A Conference on Filipino Diaspora Philanthropy," University of Santo Tomas, Manila, Philippines, June 9–10, 2005.

75. For examples of how some projects appeal to certain potential donors along these lines, compare the names and descriptions of the following organizations from the Ayala Foundation USA Approved Projects list: (1) "Defending Family Values Foundation is a non-stock, non-profit organization that aims to initiate, develop, support and sponsor all forms of programs and projects geared toward the development and preservation of family values and the dignity of human life"; (2) "Third World Movement Against the Exploitation of Women (TW-MAE-W) Direct services for sexually exploited women. An ongoing rehabilitation program for sexually abused women and children seeks to develop the self-worth of the beneficiaries as they go through the process of self-healing and renewal via education, medical and legal assistance and guidance and counseling"; (3) "Lola Grande Foundation for Women and Children, Inc. is a start- up organization that aims to advance women empowerment by promoting activities geared towards women's rights, gender responsive governance, equal human rights for women in the workplace, prevention of trafficking of women and reintegration of returning women migrants"; and (4) "North Negros Community Development Foundation, Inc. is an organization that aims to provide alternative income generation options to hundreds of sugar central and sugar farm workers in the northern part of Negros Occidental and to promote their general well-being through livelihood, education, health and nutrition programs." Ayala Foundation USA, "View Approved Projects," n.d., previously available at http://www.af-usa.org/projects.asp (accessed November 12, 2009).

76. Paul Gilroy, *Against Race: Imagining Political Culture beyond the Color Line* (Cambridge, MA: Belknap Press of Harvard University, 2000), 98.

77. See Patricia Mooney Nickel and Angela M. Eikenberg, "A Critique of the Discourse of Marketized Philanthropy," *American Behavioral Scientist* 52, no. 7 (2009): 975.

78. In particular, the lack of effective land reform, which was within President Corazon Aquino's grasp but undermined because of her family's extensive

agricultural interests, maintains the ruling elite's hold on the Philippine economy.

79. Structural adjustment in the Philippines, or the implementation of free-market policies as imposed by multilateral lending agencies, occurred in three phases that roughly corresponded with the presidencies of Marcos, Aquino, and Ramos. The emphasis during the early 1980s was on trade liberalization, the emphasis from the last years of martial law and for the Aquino administration was on debt repayment, and the emphasis through Ramos's term was on deregulation and privatization. See Walden Bello, Herbert Docena, Marissa de Guzman, and Marylou Malig, *The Anti-development State: The Political Economy of Permanent Crisis in the Philippines* (Quezon City: University of the Philippines Department of Sociology and Focus on the Global South, 2004), 12. While a severe drought in the Manila area and severe ongoing water shortages prompted Congress to grant Ramos emergency powers to enter into contracts with private corporations to address the severe lack of water access supplied by the government-run Metropolitan Waterworks and Sewerage System, the stage was clearly set for the move toward privatization by the previous three administrations. See Bello et al., *The Anti-development State*, 195, 197. Additionally, for a description of the Asian Development Bank's strategies for forcing the Philippines toward water privatization through the leveraging of loans and funds, see Freedom from Debt Coalition–Philippines, "ADB and the Privatization of Metro Manila's Water Distribution System: Corporate Greed Takes Over Public Welfare," paper presented at Regional Conference on the Asian Development Bank Water Policy, November 13–15, 2005, Quezon City, Philippines.

80. Freedom from Debt Coalition-Philippines, "ADB and the Privatization of Metro Manila's Water Distribution System," 5.

81. See Freedom from Debt Coalition–Philippines, "On the 10-Year Privatization Scheme of MWSS," paper presented to Committee on Natural Resources, House of Representatives, August 13, 2008, http://waterjustice.org/uploads/attachments/FDC%20Position%20Paper%20on%20the%2010-Year%20Privatization%20of%20MWSS%20.pdf. One 2001 report cited the increase to be from ₱2.32 (pre-privatization in 1997–1998) to ₱295. See Violeta Perez-Corral, "Monitoring MWSS-Water Rates," NGO Forum on ADB, October 2001, p. 2, https://www.yumpu.com/en/document/view/21058564/01-35-monitoring-mwss-water-rates-ngo-forum-on-adb.

82. Manila Water, "2008 Annual Report," 2008, p. 1, https://www.yumpu.com/en/document/read/39289226/manila-water-company-inc-2008-annual-report. Keep in mind that the Ayala Corporation's initial cash equity investment was sixty-seven million dollars in 1997.

83. Ibid., 31.

84. Freedom from Debt Coalition-Philippines, "On the 10-Year Privatization Scheme of MWSS," 2.

85. Bello et al., *The Anti-development State*, 195.

86. In an example of the movement to recognize water as a human right, Nils Rosemann argues the following: "The advantage of the human rights approach to basic needs, such as water, is that needs must be satisfied while human rights must be respected, protected and implemented by legal means and institutions. It is not absolutely necessary for basic needs to be satisfied by means of legal (human) rights. However, by recognising the access to safe and affordable drinking water and sufficient sanitation as a human right to water, decision-makers and state actors, whose decisions have an impact on the access and accessibility of water, are responsible for satisfying this need to the greatest possible extent. . . . The human rights approach deconstructs power relationships, such as economic and political interests, that hinder the satisfaction of basic needs. By recognising a basic need as a human right, political power is legitimized if its objective is the fulfillment of human rights, and economic power is legitimized in so far as it does not obstruct the individual or collective satisfaction of human rights." Nils Rosemann, "Financing the Human Right to Water as a Millennium Development Goal," in *Water: Global Common and Global Problems*, ed. Velma I. Glover (Enfield, NH: Science, 2006), 502.

87. Manila Water, "2008 Annual Report," 30.

88. Bello et al., *The Anti-development State*, 12.

89. Ibid., 243.

90. Ibid., 244.

91. Koike, "The Ayala Group during the Aquino Period," 442.

92. Ken Gibson, "A Case for the Family-Owned Conglomerate," *McKinsey Quarterly* 4 (2002), https://www.questia.com/library/journal/1G1-93086953/a-case-for-the-family-owned-conglomerate-the-president.

93. Alejandro Reyes and Kristina Luz, "The Elites vs. Estrada," *Asiaweek*, November 17, 2000, http://edition.cnn.com/ASIANOW/asiaweek/magazine/2000/1117/nat.philippines.html.

94. Bello et al., *The Anti-development State*, 9 (emphasis added).

95. Ibid., 287; see also Gibson, "A Case for the Family-Owned Conglomerate."

96. Bello et al., *The Anti-development State*, 244. Their most significant comparison is with South Korea. The authors also cite Thailand, Indonesia, and Malaysia, which have all reduced poverty in their countries despite ferocious corruption.

97. Ibid., 244.

98. Ibid., 298.

99. David Harvey, *A Brief History of Neoliberalism* (New York: Oxford University Press, 2005), 166.

100. For example, Victoria Garchitorena is senior adviser of the World Bank's Asia-Pacific Advisory Council against Corruption. The brothers Zobel de Ayala are signatories for the Partnering against Corruption of the World Economic Forum. The influential Makati Business Club was initiated by Enrique Zobel, chief executive officer of Ayala until 1983 and first cousin of Jaime Zobel de Ayala, and leads the Coalition against Corruption in the Philippines.

Chapter 4

1. In the diasporic response to natural disaster, I have witnessed an expressed feeling of security to giving to organizations that maintain community networks in the Philippines. Such organizations are able to rely on established relationships with organizations on the ground because one can imagine the monetary gift reaching those people suffering the most from the typhoon's destruction, those with urgent basic needs. Some smaller organizations—and even leftist or politically radical organizations—have these networks in place. Without the sense of urgency that accompanies natural disaster, smaller organizations that pursue grassroots community building do not draw the same kind of attention from Filipino American newspapers and mainstream media as they do following natural disasters. For example, the National Alliance for Filipino Concerns (NAFCON) is an action-oriented advocacy alliance concerned with Filipino welfare in the United States and with social justice and peace in the Philippines. It makes connections among militarism, environmental justice, labor trafficking in the Philippines, and immigration reform in the United States. It collaborates with leftist political organizations in the Philippines in addition to its grassroots organizing. Following Typhoon Haiyan, media organizations such as CNBC listed NAFCON's disaster relief fund alongside the Philippine Red Cross and UNICEF in its reporting.

2. See Vernadette Vicuña Gonzalez, *Securing Paradise: Tourism and Militarism in Hawai'i and the Philippines* (Durham, NC: Duke University Press, 2013).

3. Bruce Braun, *The Intemperate Rainforest: Nature, Culture, and Power on Canada's West Coast* (Minneapolis: University of Minnesota Press, 2002), 3 (emphasis in original).

4. There are two edited volumes by geographers Bruce Braun and Noel Castree that I have found particularly cogent here: Bruce Braun and Noel Castree, eds., *Remaking Reality: Nature at the Millennium* (New York: Routledge, 1998); and Noel Castree and Bruce Braun, eds., *Nature: Theory, Practice, and Politics* (Malden, MA: Blackwell, 2001).

5. Local Luxe, "Philippines Travel Guides," https://www.justluxe.com/travel/travel-guide-country.php?did=146&sub=overview (accessed October 9, 2020).

6. See Samuel P. Hays, *Explorations in Environmental History: Essays* (Pittsburgh, PA: University of Pittsburgh Press, 1998), 396.

7. As Martin Manalansan describes, Filipinos are "synonymous with the care industry across the world." Martin F. Manalansan IV, "Servicing the World: Flexible Filipinos and the Unsecured Life," in *Political Emotions*, ed. Janet Staiger, Ann Cvetkovich, and Ann Reynolds (New York: Routledge, 2010), 215.

8. Cynthia Enloe, *Bananas, Beaches, and Bases: Making Feminist Sense of International Politics* (Berkeley: University of California Press, 1989), 38.

9. Jesse Ventura, *I Ain't Got Time to Bleed: Reworking the Body Politic from the Bottom Up* (New York: Villard, 1999), 78–79, quoted in Catherine Ceniza Choy, *Empire of Care: Nursing and Migration in Filipino American History* (Durham, NC: Duke University Press, 2003), 13.

10. Vernadette V. Gonzalez, "Military Bases, 'Royalty Trips,' and Imperial Modernities: Gendered and Racialized Labor in the Postcolonial Philippines," *Frontiers* 28, no. 3 (2007): 29. See also Gonzalez, *Securing Paradise.*

11. Kevin DeLuca, "In the Shadow of Whiteness: The Consequences of Constructions of Nature in Environmental Politics," in *Whiteness: The Communication of Social Identity*, ed. Thomas K. Nakayama and Judith N. Martin (Thousand Oaks, CA: Sage, 1999), 219.

12. Rick Bonus, *Locating Filipino Americans: Ethnicity and the Cultural Politics of Space* (Philadelphia: Temple University Press, 2000), 153.

13. Ibid. Bonus also cites headlines from Filipino American community newspapers that echo these sentiments about the Philippine homeland's environmental paradise. The headlines he quotes are "Villa Escudero: Quezon's Hidden Treasure," "Breathless in Boracay," "Iloilo: The Awakening of a Sleeping Beauty," and "Cebu Remains the Queen City of the South" (153).

14. Angelo Alaan [pseudonym], interview by the author, San Francisco, CA, April 4, 2005.

15. Lonely Planet, "Philippines," https://www.lonelyplanet.com/philippines (accessed August 16, 2020).

16. Asian American studies historian Gary Y. Okihiro writes of the racialization of manliness as it was played out militarily in the American West and overseas, including in the Philippines: "Expansion and conquest, 'the white man's burden' in the words of British author Rudyard Kipling, surely helped to reconstitute a robust white masculinity. . . . [Kipling's] famous poem of that title, 'The White Man's Burden,' [was] published in 1898 to prod the United States to take up the 'burden' of empire in the Philippines." Gary Y. Okihiro, *Common Ground: Reimagining American History* (Princeton, NJ: Princeton University Press, 2001), 68.

17. For an excellent example of the application of Michael Omi and Howard Winant's racial formation theory to the project of environmental justice, see David N. Pellow and Lisa Sun-Hee Park, *The Silicon Valley of Dreams: Environmental Injustice, Immigrant Workers, and the High-Tech Global Economy* (New York: NYU Press, 2002); and Lisa Sun-Hee Park and David N. Pellow, "Racial Formation, Environmental Racism, and the Emergence of Silicon Valley," *Ethnicities* 4, no. 3 (2004): 403–423. For more on what is for some a surprisingly hostile history between the environmental movement and the environmental-justice movement, see Phaedra C. Pezzullo and Ronald Sandler, "Introduction: Revisiting the Environmental Justice Challenge to Environmentalism," in *Environmental Justice and Environmentalism: The Social Justice Challenge to the Environmental Movement*, ed. Ronald Sandler and Phaedra C. Pezzullo (Cambridge: MIT Press, 2007), 1–24.

18. U.S. General Accounting Office, "Military Base Closures: U.S. Financial Obligations in the Philippines," January 1992, p. 27, https://www.gao.gov/assets/160/151416.pdf.

19. In its notes, the U.S. General Accounting Office's report states that the average cost of construction per Superfund site is about $26 million. See ibid., 3. For the EPA's overview of CERCLA, see U.S. Environmental Protection Agency, "Superfund: CERCLA Overview," https://www.epa.gov/superfund/superfund-cercla-overview (accessed August 17, 2020).

20. Margot Laporte, "Being All It Can Be: A Solution to Improve the Department of Defense's Overseas Environmental Policy," *Duke Environmental Law and Policy Forum* 20 (Winter 2010): 219.

21. While the application of CERCLA, a piece of environmental legislation, was judged as failing to overcome the presumption of extraterritoriality, other bodies of legislation do overcome this presumption. In *ARC Ecology v. The United States Department of the Air Force*, the precedent was made for the interpretation that U.S. *environmental* laws do not extend outside its borders. However, courts show an inconsistency in the terms on the presumption of extraterritoriality as applied to *market* law such as securities and antitrust laws: "In contrast to the express congressional intent required for an environmental law to overcome the presumption, securities and antitrust laws frequently avoid the presumption, even absent a demonstration of congressional intent, because failure to apply such market laws abroad may pose a threat to the American economy. Courts have developed flexible alternatives to the presumption that allow extraterritorial application of securities and antitrust laws." See Anna D. Stasch, "ARC Ecology v. United States Department of the Air Force: Extending the Extraterritorial Reach of Domestic Environmental Law," *Environmental Law* 36 (2006): 1068.

22. Thomas L. Sansonetti, foreword to "ENRD FY 2004 Summary of Litigation Accomplishments," by U.S. Department of Justice, 2004, https://www.justice.gov/enrd/enrd-fy-2004-summary-litigation-accomplishments.

23. U.S. Department of Justice, "ENRD FY 2004 Summary."

24. Laporte, "Being All It Can Be," 221.

25. As clarified in Laporte, "Congress has the authority to enforce its laws overseas. However, courts assume that Congress legislates under a presumption against extraterritoriality. Therefore, unless Congress clearly expresses its intent to give a statute extraterritorial effect, courts assume that Congress intended the legislation to apply domestically." Ibid., 230.

26. Stasch, "ARC Ecology v. United States Department of the Air Force," 1067.

27. Valerie Kuletz, *The Tainted Desert: Environmental Ruin in the American West* (New York: Routledge, 1998), 6.

28. Ibid., 66. See also Amy Kaplan's 2003 presidential address to the American Studies Association, where this logic is also addressed: "In this logic, the

United States claims the authority to 'make sovereign judgments on what is right and what is wrong' for everyone else and 'to exempt itself with an absolutely clear conscience from all the rules that it proclaims and applies to others.' . . . If in these narratives imperial power is deemed the solution to a broken world, then they preempt any counternarratives that claim U.S. imperial actions, past and present, may have something to do with the world's problems." Amy Kaplan, "Violent Belongings and the Question of Empire Today: Presidential Address to the American Studies Association," *American Quarterly* 56, no. 1 (2004): 5–6.

29. Stephen Sandweiss, "The Social Construction of Environmental Justice," in *Environmental Injustices, Political Struggles: Race, Class, and the Environment*, ed. David E. Camacho (Durham, NC: Duke University Press, 1998), 50.

30. Galatea King, "Message from the Chair: New Directions, Building Solidarity," *Facing Justice: Quarterly News Journal of the Filipino/American Coalition for Environmental Solidarity*, Fall–Winter 2005, p. 2.

31. Ibid.

32. These quotations were originally taken from the mission statement on the FACES website but no longer appear there. They can be found in the organization's description at Great Nonprofits, "Filipino/American Coalition for Environmental Solidarity (FACES)," https://greatnonprofits.org/org/filipino-american-coalition-for-environmental-solidarity-faces (accessed October 9, 2020).

33. FACES, "Faces Program," http://www.facessolidarity.org (accessed October 9, 2020).

34. FACES board members had gone on "solidarity trips" in 2003 and 2004, but they were able to implement their redefined organizational goals on this trip in 2005.

35. Andrea Louie, "When You Are Related to the 'Other': (Re)Locating the Chinese Homeland in Asian American Politics through Cultural Tourism," *positions* 11, no. 3 (2003): 740.

36. Andrea Louie, *Chineseness across Borders: Renegotiating Chinese Identities in China and the United States* (Durham, NC: Duke University Press, 2004), 85.

37. Jake Allen [pseudonym], interview by the author, San Jose, CA, September 21, 2005.

38. FACES, "Faces Program."

39. Mariah Velasco [pseudonym], "Summary of the 2005 Face2Face Trip and Recommendations to FACES," 2005, p. 1, in the author's possession.

40. King, "Message from the Chair," 2.

41. In Tagalog, the organization name Buklod ng Kababihan connotes a bond that brings women together.

42. See the Institute for Popular Democracy's Facebook page, at https://www.facebook.com/pg/IPOPDEM/about/?ref=page_internal (accessed October 9, 2020).

43. Joel Rocamora, remarks at Face2Face Solidarity Trip, Quezon City, July 19, 2005.

44. Ramcar has been shipping lead acid batteries to Philippine Recyclers, Inc. for recycling for many years. Philippine Recyclers, Inc. denies any responsibility for the physical ailments of the local community, blaming it on leaded fuel used in cars.

45. Velasco, "Summary of the 2005 Face2Face Trip and Recommendations to FACES," 8.

46. GRO refers to "guest relations officer." In the Philippines, GRO is a popular euphemism for women who work in bars and karaoke joints and are hired to flirt with the male clientele, enticing them to purchase alcohol at inflated prices, and can often be hired for sex work in the back of the bar or off premises. While prostitution is illegal in the Philippines, the GRO industry is allowed by politicians, though for GROs and prostitutes, the "difference between the two is barely noticeable." As implied in the quotation, bars that hire GROs are predominantly found in red-light districts, such as in the area surrounding the former military base, and cater mostly to European, American, and Japanese men. Roderick T. dela Cruz, "Sex Industry Throbs with Tourism Boom," *Manila Standard*, March 28, 2006.

47. Paul Ramos [pseudonym], interview by the author, San Jose, CA, September 21, 2005.

48. Allen, interview by the author.

49. Ibid.

50. Filipino/American Coalition for Environmental Solidarity (FACES), "Preparation for 2006 Face2Face Trip," *Facing Justice: Quarterly News Journal of the Filipino/American Coalition for Environmental Solidarity*, Spring 2006, p. 4.

51. Ramos, interview by the author.

52. Paul Ramos [pseudonym], email message to the author, October 4, 2006.

Epilogue

1. Victor Velasquez [pseudonym], interview by the author, Angono, Rizal, Philippines, February 1, 2006.

Index

L. Joyce Zapanta Mariano is an Associate Professor of American Studies at the University of Hawai'i at Mānoa.

ALSO IN THE SERIES *ASIAN AMERICAN HISTORY AND CULTURE*:

Jiemin Bao, *Creating a Buddhist Community: A Thai Temple in Silicon Valley*
Elda E. Tsou, *Unquiet Tropes: Form, Race, and Asian American Literature*
Tarry Hum, *Making a Global Immigrant Neighborhood: Brooklyn's Sunset Park*
Ruth Mayer, *Serial Fu Manchu: The Chinese Supervillain and the Spread of Yellow Peril Ideology*
Karen Kuo, *East Is West and West Is East: Gender, Culture, and Interwar Encounters between Asia and America*
Kieu-Linh Caroline Valverde, *Transnationalizing Viet Nam: Community, Culture, and Politics in the Diaspora*
Lan P. Duong, *Treacherous Subjects: Gender, Culture, and Trans-Vietnamese Feminism*
Kristi Brian, *Reframing Transracial Adoption: Adopted Koreans, White Parents, and the Politics of Kinship*
Belinda Kong, *Tiananmen Fictions outside the Square: The Chinese Literary Diaspora and the Politics of Global Culture*
Bindi V. Shah, *Laotian Daughters: Working toward Community, Belonging, and Environmental Justice*
Cherstin M. Lyon, *Prisons and Patriots: Japanese American Wartime Citizenship, Civil Disobedience, and Historical Memory*
Shelley Sang-Hee Lee, *Claiming the Oriental Gateway: Prewar Seattle and Japanese America*
Isabelle Thuy Pelaud, *This Is All I Choose to Tell: History and Hybridity in Vietnamese American Literature*
Christian Collet and Pei-te Lien, eds., *The Transnational Politics of Asian Americans*
Min Zhou, *Contemporary Chinese America: Immigration, Ethnicity, and Community Transformation*
Kathleen S. Yep, *Outside the Paint: When Basketball Ruled at the Chinese Playground*
Benito M. Vergara Jr., *Pinoy Capital: The Filipino Nation in Daly City*
Jonathan Y. Okamura, *Ethnicity and Inequality in Hawai'i*
Sucheng Chan and Madeline Y. Hsu, eds., *Chinese Americans and the Politics of Race and Culture*
K. Scott Wong, *Americans First: Chinese Americans and the Second World War*
Lisa Yun, *The Coolie Speaks: Chinese Indentured Laborers and African Slaves in Cuba*

Estella Habal, *San Francisco's International Hotel: Mobilizing the Filipino American Community in the Anti-eviction Movement*

Thomas P. Kim, *The Racial Logic of Politics: Asian Americans and Party Competition*

Sucheng Chan, ed., *The Vietnamese American 1.5 Generation: Stories of War, Revolution, Flight, and New Beginnings*

Antonio T. Tiongson Jr., Edgardo V. Gutierrez, and Ricardo V. Gutierrez, eds., *Positively No Filipinos Allowed: Building Communities and Discourse*

Sucheng Chan, ed., *Chinese American Transnationalism: The Flow of People, Resources, and Ideas between China and America during the Exclusion Era*

Rajini Srikanth, *The World Next Door: South Asian American Literature and the Idea of America*

Keith Lawrence and Floyd Cheung, eds., *Recovered Legacies: Authority and Identity in Early Asian American Literature*

Linda Trinh Võ, *Mobilizing an Asian American Community*

Franklin S. Odo, *No Sword to Bury: Japanese Americans in Hawai'i during World War II*

Josephine Lee, Imogene L. Lim, and Yuko Matsukawa, eds., *Re/collecting Early Asian America: Essays in Cultural History*

Linda Trinh Võ and Rick Bonus, eds., *Contemporary Asian American Communities: Intersections and Divergences*

Sunaina Marr Maira, *Desis in the House: Indian American Youth Culture in New York City*

Teresa Williams-León and Cynthia Nakashima, eds., *The Sum of Our Parts: Mixed-Heritage Asian Americans*

Tung Pok Chin with Winifred C. Chin, *Paper Son: One Man's Story*

Amy Ling, ed., *Yellow Light: The Flowering of Asian American Arts*

Rick Bonus, *Locating Filipino Americans: Ethnicity and the Cultural Politics of Space*

Darrell Y. Hamamoto and Sandra Liu, eds., *Countervisions: Asian American Film Criticism*

Martin F. Manalansan IV, ed., *Cultural Compass: Ethnographic Explorations of Asian America*

Ko-lin Chin, *Smuggled Chinese: Clandestine Immigration to the United States*

Evelyn Hu-DeHart, ed., *Across the Pacific: Asian Americans and Globalization*

Soo-Young Chin, *Doing What Had to Be Done: The Life Narrative of Dora Yum Kim*

Robert G. Lee, *Orientals: Asian Americans in Popular Culture*

David L. Eng and Alice Y. Hom, eds., *Q & A: Queer in Asian America*

K. Scott Wong and Sucheng Chan, eds., *Claiming America: Constructing Chinese American Identities during the Exclusion Era*

Lavina Dhingra Shankar and Rajini Srikanth, eds., *A Part, Yet Apart: South Asians in Asian America*

Jere Takahashi, *Nisei/Sansei: Shifting Japanese American Identities and Politics*

Velina Hasu Houston, ed., *But Still, Like Air, I'll Rise: New Asian American Plays*

Josephine Lee, *Performing Asian America: Race and Ethnicity on the Contemporary Stage*

Deepika Bahri and Mary Vasudeva, eds., *Between the Lines: South Asians and Postcoloniality*

E. San Juan Jr., *The Philippine Temptation: Dialectics of Philippines–U.S. Literary Relations*

Carlos Bulosan and E. San Juan Jr., eds., *The Cry and the Dedication*

Carlos Bulosan and E. San Juan Jr., eds., *On Becoming Filipino: Selected Writings of Carlos Bulosan*

Vicente L. Rafael, ed., *Discrepant Histories: Translocal Essays on Filipino Cultures*

Yen Le Espiritu, *Filipino American Lives*

Paul Ong, Edna Bonacich, and Lucie Cheng, eds., *The New Asian Immigration in Los Angeles and Global Restructuring*

Chris Friday, *Organizing Asian American Labor: The Pacific Coast Canned-Salmon Industry, 1870–1942*

Sucheng Chan, ed., *Hmong Means Free: Life in Laos and America*

Timothy P. Fong, *The First Suburban Chinatown: The Remaking of Monterey Park, California*

William Wei, *The Asian American Movement*

Yen Le Espiritu, *Asian American Panethnicity*

Velina Hasu Houston, ed., *The Politics of Life*

Renqiu Yu, *To Save China, To Save Ourselves: The Chinese Hand Laundry Alliance of New York*

Shirley Geok-lin Lim and Amy Ling, eds., *Reading the Literatures of Asian America*

Karen Isaksen Leonard, *Making Ethnic Choices: California's Punjabi Mexican Americans*

Gary Y. Okihiro, *Cane Fires: The Anti-Japanese Movement in Hawaii, 1865–1945*

Sucheng Chan, *Entry Denied: Exclusion and the Chinese Community in America, 1882–1943*